MW00714490

WHEN WOMEN
CONNECT

WHEN WOMEN CONNECT

Extraordinary Stories of Sisterhood and Solid Advice for Finding Meaningful Connections

A Stepping Into Victory Compilation: Volume 2

Tymm Publishing LLC

Columbia, SC

When Women Connect: Extraordinary Stories of
Sisterhood and Solid Advice for Finding Meaningful
Connections

A Stepping Into Victory Compilation: Volume 2

Paperback ISBN: 978-0-9984569-8-0
Ebook ISBN: 978-0-9984569-9-7

Published by Tymm Publishing LLC
701 Gervais Street, Suite 150-185
Columbia, SC 29201
www.tymmpublishing.com

Cover Design: TywebbinCreations.com
Editing: Felicia Murrell

DEDICATION

This book is dedicated to a few of my friends and mentors over the years.

Connie, Mimi and Salli, for being more than co-workers. It's been quite the journey.

Robin, who helped me grow as a writer and mentored me through this author journey from the very beginning.

Debra, Eula, Sandra, Alice, Ernestine, Annette, Annie, and Jenny, I appreciate the friendship and count it a blessing to be among military wives who've stood firm in faith. Thanks to you, I grew into the woman I am today.

~ Tyora Moody, Compilation Editor

CONTENTS

PART II.
HOW TO MAKE MEANINGFUL CONNECTIONS

ACKNOWLEDGEMENTS

The idea behind the Stepping into Victory compilations has grown. I felt like there were "real" stories to be told and couldn't let go of creating a platform for a nonfiction series as a spin-off to a fiction series. I'm excited that this compilation is dedicated to friendships, mentors and all other forms of sisterhood in a woman's life.

I want to thank Robin Caldwell and Valerie J. Lewis Coleman who assisted me with learning how to pull together compilations. This one has truly been a pleasure to compile. A huge thanks to Felicia Murrell for her patient editing of each co-author's chapter.

This anthology would not exist without the contributions of the following: Angelia White, Arnita L. Fields, Denise Kelley, Brenda Johnson, Michelle Spady, Yvette Wilson Bentley, Renee Spivey, Madlyn Marshall, Jeanette Hill, Dawn McCoy, Linda Leigh Hargrove, and Audrey Tyler.

The transparency and willingness to share your friendships and mentors has inspired me and I pray it will inspire the readers of this book.

FOREWORD

ANGELIA WHITE

As women, we face too many struggles and moments of pain throughout our lives to count. The last thing we need is added stress and hurt brought on by other women. Rather than tearing each other apart, we need to build one another up so we can tear down walls *together*.

I've had my fair share of ups and downs in my own life, and you know what one of the most powerful forces was that helped me walk when I could barely crawl? *My tribe of incredible women.* Whether it was women in my family or my circle of friends or those who walked alongside me as my mentors, I've been fortunate enough to have a number of amazing women show me what it means to be genuine and strong.

When I heard about *When Women Connect*, I knew it was going to be something I could immediately get behind. Its message and intention are in line with what we publish in *Hope for Women*, the magazine I started more than thirteen years ago. I love how this book encourages and challenges women to seek deep and meaningful connections in their lives and to be in community with other women seeking the same.

Ladies, we are not meant to do life alone. Surround yourself with women who will support you and remind you of who you are and why your dreams matter. Those are the women who will be there for you when it feels like the rest of the world has turned its back on you.

When Women Connect is the perfect reminder that we need to be in connection with one another on a consistent basis. I'm so proud of my dear friend Tyora and her insight in this work, and I can't wait for others to be able to learn from the wisdom she shares.

Let's keep building each other up, and let's keep forming those connections that change your life in ways you never could have imagined.

INTRODUCTION

TYORA MOODY

If you're not familiar with the Stepping into Victory Compilations, this nonfiction series is considered a spin-off to a fiction series. I know that sounds weird! When I was editing the third and final book in the Victory Gospel Series, this idea formed to reach out to real women.

Each one of the main characters in the books, Candace – *When Rain Falls*, Angel – *When Memories Fade* and Lenora – *When Perfection Fails* were female entrepreneurs. Not only were they entrepreneurs, but they all attended the fictional Victory Gospel Church, even attending the same bible study. There is sometimes a hint of an author's life within their stories. I've always enjoyed connecting with other women who have similar interests and personalities which is exactly what happens to these three women over the course of three books.

The world wide web is full of opportunities to meet people. As an introvert, it's probably been my main source of meeting new people in the past decade. The various platforms can be overwhelming, so it's important to proceed with caution but to keep an open mind.

On the flip side, I also like to connect people to each other. I'm a listener and like to provide solutions, when requested. It's a regular occurrence to find inquiries in my inbox, voicemails, texts and the various social media messengers. Depending on the goal of the person making the request, I carefully consider if I can help them or if I know of another person who would make a better connection. There is a sense of joy when both parties return back to me with the success of connection.

A few years ago, while working on the compilation, *When Women Become Business Owner*, it occurred to me after reading the co-authors' stories, how many of these women I had personally connected with over the years. Many of them I encountered early on when my business was new and I was still trying to figure out what I was doing. I, in turn, also watched them grow with their own businesses. We talked on the phone for hours, sharing and brainstorming ideas, and over the years, I have had the opportunity to meet a few in person. There's nothing quite like connecting the avatar on social media with the person.

Still with all the connections I've made over the years, there remains a handful of women who have my deepest trust. Who know the real me behind the smile. I think this is normal with most women, that they keep a few close friends or even one main BFF.

Our lives are shaped by the women we come in contact with throughout our lives. These women can be our mothers, aunts, grandmothers, sisters, friends or co-workers. Many women are wounded by the ugly, shallow conflicts that burst forth from other women who've let their own insecurities rule their behavior. Unfortunately, once pain is inflicted, grudges, mistrust and unforgiveness can reign too long, not allowing for the chance for deeper connections.

If a person is sucked into the world of reality television, whether the *Housewives* series, *Basketball Wives*, *Love & Hip-Hop*, the viewer may forget the desire for ratings overrides the common decency of how women should treat each other. I say ignore that superficial world.

When Women Connect strives to highlight and encourage women to reach for deeper connections in their lives. In Part One, the co-authors share stories of extraordinary connections that led to unlikely friendships and unforgettable mentors. For women who are seeking ways to make better connections, co-authors from Part Two offer advice that can transcend any place, whether it be home, church, or work.

PART I

EXTRAORDINARY STORIES OF SISTERHOOD

1

COVENANT SISTERHOOD

ARNITA L. FIELDS

"Two are better than one, because they have a good return on their labor. If either of them falls down, one can help the other up. But pity anyone who falls and has no one to help them up. Also, if two lie down together, they will keep warm. But how can one keep warm alone? Though one may be overpowered, two can defend themselves. A cord of three strands is not quickly broken." *Ecclesiastes 4:9-12 NIV*

∞

Authentic covenant sisterhood made a life changing impact in my life. But before I tell you my story, I would like to share with you what covenant and sisterhood mean. The word covenant is derived from the Hebrew word *berith* which occurred in the Old Testament over 250 times. Although there have been many debates over the years concerning the true definition of the word *covenant*, several online dictionaries describe it as:

- A usually formal, solemn and binding agreement.

- A written agreement or promise usually under seal between two or more parties especially for the performance of some action.

- An agreement between two parties to do or not to do something.

The word *sisterhood* can be defined as:

- The state of being a sister.

- Sisterly relationship.

- A community or society of sisters;

especially: a society of women in a religious order.

- The solidarity of women based on shared conditions, experiences or concerns.

One of the most beautiful and fruitful covenant connections I have been blessed to have came during one of my lowest points in life. On time as He always is, God sent a dear sister, Tanya whom I met at church when I lived in Nashville, Tennessee. After meeting, we became fast friends. We were both worshippers of God, loved to read, enjoyed relaxing music and so such more. Since we both worked in buildings not far from each other in downtown Nashville, we would meet up for lunch from time to time or stop to chat during the course of our busy days.

The beauty of our connection was that I could be perfectly open about myself, my struggles as well as my fears. Honestly, we both were able to be open and transparent about anything. To me, she was truly an authentic, covenant sister God blessed me with during the time I most needed this type of relationship.

Tanya and I started and ended our two-and-a-half-year minister's training together. On the evening we would preach our first sermonette, we practiced together before going to the church to minister before our pastor and peers. She felt called to work with the youth and I was called to work in counseling married couples. In class, we sat next to each other, discussed lessons and prayed for each other when we thought we would not make it to the end of our training period. We corrected each other in love when we were off track, challenged each other with the truth of God's word, and pushed each other to excel, dream big and press into the greatness God had placed within us as individuals, wives to our husband's, mothers to our children and as committed and submitted vessels to Him.

When I moved back to Memphis, she was one of the people I knew I would miss the most. While I had other covenant sisters during my stay, I always felt divinely strengthened and empowered after the conversations she and I shared.

I returned to Memphis in August 2004, the same year we graduated from ministry school. Tanya and I had talked and prayed about my move back. A few years later, I was notified my friend and covenant sister had passed away. I was shaken to my core. I had lost a sister, friend, coach, mentor, counselor, prayer partner, and confidant. Our four-year friendship held more substance than many of the relationships I ever had. God allowed His precious daughter to leave such a huge deposit and make a life changing impact upon my life. And to this day, I know our meeting was a divine appointment to help me through my life transition and trials.

In 2009, I was asked to deliver a message during an online women's conference. As I reflected on my covenant relationship with Tanya and many others like her whom the Father divinely yet strategically brought across my path, I began to cry and thanked Him for those who had demonstrated His heart for me. I then sat down and birthed the message God gave me concerning authentic covenant sisterhood. Later that night, during the online conference, it was prophesied that God would give me a book to help women. I was tickled because the message for the conference had become the outline for *Covenant Sisterhood: Embracing Heaven's Divine Connection* which teaches women how to embrace the authentic covenant relationships God has called for them to walk in with other women.

Take a few moments to reflect on an authentic covenant sisterhood relationship you have had an opportunity to experience and enjoy throughout your life. Here are a few questions you can use to guide your reflection.

- *What were some of the unique things about this relationship that stand out the most to you?*
- *What were some of the character traits that made your covenant sister different from others?*
- *What are some of the things that you personally deposited to enhance your covenant relationship?*
- *Have you ever walked away prematurely from a true covenant relationship?*
- *What was the reason behind your departure?*
- *Was the relationship restored? Yes or No? If no, why not?*

May you be encouraged and strengthened by the words shared in this poem and covenant renewal prayer written for *Covenant Sisterhood: Embracing Heaven's Divine Connection.*

∞

COVENANT SISTERHOOD

(Sisters United)

Sisters on the rise and on the move,
casting down impure motives
because we have kingdom work to do.
Sisters on the rise and on the move,
we are not like the sisters of our past
because God has created in us something new.
Sisters on the rise and on the move,
our hearts knit together in Christian love;
So people can see Jesus in us through and
through.
Sisters on the rise and on the move,
connecting our gifts together in perfect harmony
as divinely connected covenant sisters should do.

© 2009 by Arnita L. Fields

∞

COVENANT RENEWAL PRAYER

Father God, we come before you humbling our hearts and aligning our minds with you and your divine will. We ask that you first create in us a clean heart and purify us that we may be vessels unto honor, meet for the master's use. We cast down our cares and lay them at the feet of Jesus. We repent of holding bitterness, strife, envy, jealousy and anger in the crevices of our hearts. We ask that you forgive us for allowing offenses to take our focus off of you and what you have purposed for us to do. May we recognize the enemy for who he really is. May our eyes be open to see through your eyes and with your perspective. May our way of thinking be elevated above every circumstance and every problem we come against. May our hearts become pure before you as we work together to see your will performed in the earth. Not our will, but your will be done in the earth as it has already been firmly established in heaven. May your purpose be continually revealed as we seek you daily for instruction and wisdom. May our hearts burn with passion to complete what you have begun in us.

Father God, we thank you for reminding us of what true covenant relationships represent, and we honor you for strategically setting up those divine connections that can only come from you.

Revive, restore and renew those covenant relationships we walked away from prematurely.

Forgive us for breaking confidence and covenant with the sisters you had divinely connected us to. May we recognize and understand that these relationships are not about us but are about fulfilling your purpose in the earth.

May we walk in love and treat our covenant sisters with honor, dignity and respect. May we walk in integrity and peace with those you have divinely connected us to. And, Father God, we ask that you bless our covenant relationships with your mercy, grace and power.

We honor you now for all you have done, and for all you will do through our submitted and committed vessels.

Thank you for the grace to finish the course that has been set before us. Thank you for the opportunity and privilege to represent you as kingdom ambassadors. We will not be ashamed of the gospel of Jesus Christ for we will walk in holy boldness to bring both glory and honor to your mighty name.

May the words of our mouth and the meditation of our hearts be pleasing and acceptable in your sight; O God, our Lord, and our redeemer, in Jesus' name, we pray. Amen.

ABOUT THE AUTHOR

Milwaukee, Wisconsin native, **Arnita L. Fields** is a wife and Christian counselor. As a passionate advocate for emotionally healthy covenant marriages, she was inspired to write the book series, *After the Affair: Emotional Healing God's Way* to help covenant couples heal after a physical or emotional affair.

In addition to being an award-winning author, she is a graduate of Regent University with a Master of Arts in Human Services Counseling. Arnita and her husband, Anthony, have been married twenty-one years and currently call Memphis, Tennessee, home. If you would like to contact Arnita, you may send an email to arnitafields@yahoo.com or visit her website at arnitalfields.info.

2

THE
UNEXPECTED
CONNECTION

DENISE A. KELLEY

The thief comes only to steal, and kill, and destroy
~ John 10:10(a), NASB ~

Confidante: One to whom secrets are entrusted;
especially one who is a woman.

∞

It's been said true friendship between women are impossible without all the *cattiness* and drama. I will not deny, in some circumstances, that stereotype holds true. I can also attest that is not the case in all situations. It's very refreshing to encounter connections where that assumption is proven false.

I am a Christian. Therefore, I approach issues in my life from a Christian perspective. First, I'll begin by saying: **NEWSFLASH!** Guess what? Friendships are okay. It doesn't stop there, I have more exciting news. Guess what? GOD is okay with you having friends. It's not abnormal that as you *do* life, you will engage, some time or another, in relationships that will not always work out.

The demise of a friendship could be for various reasons; you may find out something you're not able to handle or something is revealed about you the other party doesn't want to deal with. For whatever reason, it becomes a prime opportunity for satan to present himself. In this place, he will attempt to plant seeds of *isolation*. This seed will cause you to *withdraw* and keep to yourself in order to avoid repeating your last *friendship* mistake. He will also take this opportunity to plant *fear*. This seed will cause you not to trust another person. An internal wall is built to keep people out. Unfortunately, it doesn't stop there, satan will also plant *doubt*. This seed will cause you to *not* engage or embrace new friendships because you doubt the authenticity of the union.

The enemy is waiting patiently for your times of disappointment and hurt. You must always remember and understand he is an opportunist. When he sees you at a weak point, he will infiltrate and do all he can to pull you away from everyone. He wants to get you alone in order to penetrate and distort your thoughts, which in turn will determine how you're going to react. It's also in this place, even if someone genuinely expresses their desire to pursue a friendship, due to past events, you doubt and question their motives. Isolation, fear, and doubt doesn't begin to scrape the surface of satan's techniques. The truth is, when devastating things happen, it potentially leaves a trail of negative behavior as well as a negative outlook. He will try to make you believe you don't need friends and are better off alone. In a nutshell, satan will pour all types of harmful and negative thoughts in your mind.

The thought pattern of *you don't need anyone* is a trick from the enemy. More importantly, that's not GOD'S design for his children. The answer is not to avoid and shut people out. Abandoning the sanctity and union of friendship does not render the best decision. The Bible supports divine connections. Therefore, you should consult the

Lord about who you allow to be part of your life and who you are friends with.

FRIENDS (THE BIBLE STORY)

A friend loves at all times, and a brother is there for times of trouble. ~Prov. 17:17, ISV~

After witnessing the bravery of David, King Saul asked his commander who was David's father. The commander didn't know but rushed to find out. The commander returned with David holding the head of the giant, Goliath in his hand. Jonathan, King Saul's son was nearby as David and his father conversed. After David finished speaking with King Saul, the soul of David and Jonathan were knit together. They instantly bonded together in friendship and brotherhood. Jonathan was next in line to inherit the kingdom which his father ruled over, but Jonathan knew otherwise. He knew David was destined to be king, and he was okay with that. Jonathan and David's friendship was draped in covenant. Although Jonathan's father wanted David killed, even that didn't damage their friendship. Jonathan knew in his heart of hearts he wouldn't rule as king, and his bond with David remained untouched. Up until the day David fled the kingdom in order to save his life from Jonathan's father, their friendship remained intact.

Jonathan and David loved each other as if they were *blood* brothers. Matter of fact, blood couldn't have made them any closer. This friendship possessed qualities of a solid relationship. Their friendship was based on trust, loyalty and love, which instantly transitioned into *brotherhood*.

WHEN WOMEN CONNECT (MY STORY)

Iron sharpens iron, and one man sharpens another
~Proverbs 27:17, ESV~

Regrettably, I've experienced the misfortune of having friendships fall apart. I've also been fortunate enough to have a few close sisterhood/ friendships and deciding who to write about, for this collection of stories, became a daunting task. To narrow down my selection process, I chose my most recent divine connection, but let me ask you a question.

Have you ever met someone who was simply *good people?*

∞

In November 2015, around the time my church, Greater Prayer Temple Ministries, held our Elevation Conference, I met someone who was simply *good people*. This was an exciting time for my church and everyone anticipated the services. This was a three-day event with speakers from all over. We'd invited speakers from New York to Georgia. All the speakers were individuals we've never heard preach before, and that was another thing we were anticipating. We were prepared to meet and connect with new people.

The day finally arrived, and the guests started pouring in earlier that day with the exception of one of our speakers. Unfortunately, he'd encountered an emergency and was unable to attend. At first, we weren't quite sure how we were going to replace him at the last minute, but GOD worked it out, as he always does. Apostle Valecia Tigner was scheduled to speak the following night, but graciously agreed to also speak in place of the absentee preacher. The congregation fell in love with her immediately. She's an anointed woman of GOD with poise, style and grace. It was a treat to get to hear her for two nights. Although Apostle Tigner holds a high position in the church, she is approachable. After the conference, she greeted everyone and became acquainted. The women's department decided to invite her back for our women's conference as the keynote speaker. Apostle Tigner accepted the invitation without hesitation and just like that she was scheduled to come back in six months.

I knew this was the start of a new connection for my church, but I didn't know the Lord also destined for this to be a new personal sisterhood connection of my own. Prior to her coming back to do our women's conference, I would check on her from time to time via social media; still not realizing GOD was building a connection. One day, I received an unexpected inbox message on Facebook from Apostle Tigner. The Lord dropped me in her spirit. He'd given her words of prophecy as well as encouragement on my behalf. After reading the message, I thanked GOD for thinking of me and placing me on someone's heart to speak *good* things into my life. At this point, I still wasn't fully aware of the connection, but I knew GOD was in it.

As time passed, it was clear this wasn't *happenstance*, but a divine connection orchestrated by GOD. There were a few things that brought this revelation to light, but one main thing was a determining factor. May arrived and during our women's conference, Apostle Tigner seized the opportunity to minister individually to most of the ladies in the church. Without knowing anything about me, the words GOD gave her to release to me was *just* what I needed at the time. There was a situation heavy on my mind, but I came to church with a smile on my face in spite of. Apostle Tigner was able to discern something wasn't *quite right*. In passing, she asked if I was okay. Of course, I said yes, I was fine while smiling and nodding my head. She said, *"I'm not going to push the issue, but I'm feeling something is wrong."* I chuckled. But in that moment, I realized this was the handiwork of GOD.

Up until this point, our method of communication was social media or through her church administrators. We did not have each other's personal contact information. Before leaving this time, she gave me her personal contact information in case I needed to get in touch with her instead of communicating through social media. I was honored and considered that a privilege. Although she's not much older than me, her experience, knowledge, and more importantly, her connection with GOD affords me the opportunity at any given moment to glean from her nuggets of wisdom and words of prophecy. In the short span we've known each other, there has been times when I had to endure a *hard truth*. Even in that, she delivers it in love, and I can tell she has my best interest at heart. There have been other times, when a lesson needed to be revealed or taught. These are what she calls *teachable moments*. In these *teachable moments*, I've gained knowledge on friendships, relationships, life nuggets, and spiritual revelation. Our affiliation is not a struggle or uncomfortable. We've discussed becoming business partners, plans to get her book completed, ways to grow/enhance her personal ministry, and a number of other positive things. GOD has allowed our friendship to have a natural flow. It feels like we've known each other for years.

Apostle Tigner is very selective about who she allows in her *inner circle* due to who she is in the Kingdom and where the Lord is taking her. She's not only an apostle, but also has her own church. She's been a pastor for over twenty years, and anything that's not GOD ordained, she's not going to entertain. With that in mind, I don't take it lightly she's entrusted me in her space.

As I often say, GOD is strategic. When I take

time to really think about the turn of events, GOD connected us at a good time. I was going through a *breakdown* of a long-standing friendship. This individual had been my *sisterfriend* for many years, but within the past year we'd been clashing. It didn't feel much like the sisterhood it had been for the past seventeen years. The moment it began to become too much, in comes Apostle Tigner.

She has proven to be trustworthy, genuine and sincere. In December 2017, those qualities hit home for me as tragedy visited. My father was sent home on hospice and died a week and a half later on December 23, 2017. Apostle Tigner was scheduled to come back to my church and do our year end revival, but offered to come to Virginia a few days earlier in case my family needed help with anything. I told her that wouldn't be necessary, but her offer was greatly appreciated. When it came time for my father's funeral, Apostle Tigner was in Virginia preparing for my church's conference. She came prepared to attend the funeral, although she'd never met my father. Once again, she volunteered her service and time without reservation. I assured her again my family didn't need anything. I didn't want to interrupt her study and preparation time, so I told her she didn't have to attend the funeral. Her willingness to *make* herself available was another sign of GOD building a connection.

The other beautiful thing about this story is GOD didn't stop there with just connecting Apostle Tigner and myself. I've also established friendships with a few others in her church. When they received the news of my father's passing, they also inquired about helping.

Due to failed friendships, I was apprehensive with engaging in *new* friendships. The Lord revealed godly friendships are good to have. In the past, I made the mistake of not allowing the Holy Ghost to steer me in the right direction when it came to my selection of friends. For that reason, I shut down. After a while, the Lord revealed he didn't intend for us to *do life* alone. Divine connections from GOD will reap a benefit in more ways than one. As the Lord was bringing me out of my *state of seclusion*, he had me focus on one verse.

A man that hath friends must shew himself friendly...
~Proverbs 18:24(a), KJV~

I made a conscious decision. I was ready to welcome new friendships, but only if they were

GOD ordained. It was at that time the *association* with Apostle Tigner unexpectedly evolved into a *friendship*. It went from *"just sending you a message to check on you"* to *"whenever you're in Georgia, you are welcome in my home."* The Lord's purpose for this divine connection is not completely clear. The friendship is still unfolding, but I know it is GOD's doing. I'm grateful GOD has allowed our paths to cross. I'm excited to see GOD's ultimate plan for this connection as I continue on this friendship journey.

ABOUT THE AUTHOR

Denise Kelley is a freelance writer whose love for writing and reading began at a young age. She writes Urban Christian fiction, which she brings to life whether she's writing poetry, novels or plays. Denise's Christian plays have been performed in various locations in her local community.

Denise has a short story featured in *The Motherhood Diaries 2*, by National Bestseller, ReShonda Tate Billingsley. Her debut novel entitled: *70×7: The Road to Forgiveness* was originally released in 2014; but has since been relaunched with Anointed Inspirations Publishing in 2016. The new title is *Even When It Hurts: Seventy Times Seven*. This novel received a Five Star review. On release date the novel was number one on Amazon's kindle list as a Hot New Release for Urban Christian Fiction. Denise was also number two on Amazon's Kindle list for Best Seller. Denise's released a novella entitled: *Revenge: Sweet as Cain* in Dec. 2015. This novella also received a five star review from PEN 'Ashe magazine.

Denise has co-authored in several anthologies

to encourage women. She recently co-authored in the project RELEASE by Saba Tekle.

She can be contacted at daknovelist@gmail.com or her Facebook fan page, Author D. A. Kelley.

3

FRIENDSHIP DISCOVERED IN UNLIKELY PLACES

MICHELLE SPADY AND BRENDA JOHNSON

Once upon a time there were two women of diverse backgrounds whose paths crossed at a little, white church on a hill in Virginia. It has often been said that with God and religion, "all things are possible". This philosophy on friendship has never been truer than in our case. Because of our diverse backgrounds and upbringing, it is highly unlikely that our paths would have ever crossed anywhere other than

31

inside a church. Ours is not a friendship that was formed from our childhood or college days, but more so from situations we've both encountered over the years evolving from what we believe is our own personal Christian walk and life's journey. This friendship and walk with Christ has inspired us to write a book together to encourage other women to have faith and trust in each other and God. We both realize the importance of a good, solid friendship, and we also realize that many people take friends for granted. For that reason, we have agreed to share some of our secrets for solidifying and maintaining our friendship, as well as a few from others who've written books on the topic.

You're invited to enjoy this true story of friendship as each of us shares what our friendship means to us from our own personal perspective and the foundation from which it was built. You will be surprised at what can bring two entirely different people together. Ours is a bond that works for us, but at the same time can serve as a template for others to follow when forming and sustaining uniquely created friendships and relationships that go against the odds. We don't always see eye-to-eye on every situation, but we would give an eye-for-an eye for some of the same things in life. While reading our definitions and expressions of friendship, it is our hope that you will find some nugget you can take away to help you to build, develop and nurture a 'Christ-like' friendship with someone. Above all, we hope you will see our amity for our faith, love and trust of God.

Until this writing, we have never expressed how or what we think of each other. Read for the true meaning of friendship in the eyes of the beholder and how our two paths merged with God at the center. "From here on out, in honor of our grandmothers, we will refer to ourselves as "Wilma" (Michelle) and "Pennie Mae" (Brenda).

∞

Wilma: Respect and education were two things that were expected and required in our family. Love (amidst the chaos) was there, but not outwardly expressed. Though my family were Christians, giving and loving, they were not the type of family who outwardly expressed it. Growing up, I often envied friends whose parents gave them a hug and a kiss on their way out the door. Dysfunction amuck, through silent consent we knew we were loved. Over time, my siblings and I have learned to show expressions of love towards each other. Because I experienced a different kind of unconditional love, friendships outside of family are still different for me. I can be very distant when it comes to letting people know how I feel about them, and this type of personality can be hard for creating and building friendships and relationships with people. Pennie Mae mentions these types of relationships in her descriptions of friends. I've worked on this personality trait as I've grown. People privileged to know me 'up close and personal', say I have a very "BIG" heart. I inherited that from my mother. I show my likes and dislikes for people in unique ways, though not often verbally.

Pennie Mae: My family was a loving family. My mom and dad didn't say, "I love you" all the time either. But somehow, I knew from their actions that they loved me and my siblings dearly. Growing up, I guess I was considered an introvert, very shy and yes, naïve. I grew up in a very small town on a farm in Mississippi. At one point, both of my grandparents lived on the same farm. Right across the road, we'd say. We worked hard for what we had, and we were taught to be proud of our family heritage. We were expected to work on the farm, finish school and get a good education. Not going to college was not an option. I knew that whatever the sacrifice, my dad and mom were going to make it. My mom and dad were strict; we could not spend the night away from home. Even though we could not spend the night away from home, my mom would let our friends come over and spend the night on occasion. It was fun, and our house seemed to be full all the time, especially after church on Sunday. I have friends I grew up with and many others over the years that are still my friends.

Wilma: One day I was invited to a "little white church on the hill" as it is so affectionately referred to. It was a very small church with history. Last year, it celebrated one hundred and forty-five years of ministry. For me, that says a lot about an institution of any kind, especially a church. I found this church to be very intimate. The church was undergoing building renovations, and many of the members were not present. I believe the small congregation contributed to the spiritual bonds and friendships that were formed. The size allowed members more of an opportunity to get to know one another on a personal level that would have been impossible in a larger church. It was there that I met my good friend, "Pennie Mae".

Many people search for years to find someone they can call a true friend. Probably because true blue friends are rare gems. Friends have been defined as people who share mutual affection towards each other. Someone you can rely on. Your BFF. Your ride or die. Just to name a few. Merriam Webster dictionary defines friends as "one attached to another by affection or esteem; one that is not hostile; or one that favors or promotes something. A few of these apply to us. As Tom Hanks said in the movie Forest Gump, "Mama always said life is like a box of chocolates, you never know what you're gonna get." I didn't know what I'd get with Pennie Mae.

What we share did not come overnight, but with time, the trust in our friendship grew. I learned to trust Pennie Mae. She was once a stranger who became familiar over time. Some say a good friend is like a good book. The inside is better than the cover. This is Pennie Mae. I know I can count on her support whenever I need it, and I value our talks. She is a source of calm and comfort. She is like another quote that I've heard about women's friendships and relationships.

"One would say that friends are like bras, close to your heart and there to support." I know that what I share with Pennie Mae won't go anywhere. These types of relationships are a dying breed. I can rely on her to give me an honest, unbiased opinion about something and count on her to think about it before she makes a promise. "Promises are the glue of relationships."

Through the years, I have considered myself insecure, almost afraid at times, shy, not worthy, lacking in confidence, of low self-esteem, very impulsive and sometimes uptight. Pennie Mae is the antithesis of me, bringing encouragement and strength. And yet, in some ways, we are a lot alike. If asked to describe her, I'd say she is kind, patient, very welcoming, can be outgoing, playful, cheerful, very protective of what she loves and cares about, but at the same time naïve about some of the things I've been through or believe to be true. She's always there when I need to vent or need a logical and practical approach to a situation. She offers positivity and sincerity; qualities that can help make a person's life more bearable. Pennie Mae brings the logical side to our friendship. She doesn't get offended when you get a second opinion, and regardless of what I may want to hear, she will give me the truth.

Pennie Mae: Insecure is never a word I would use for Wilma. She is always willing to take a risk, especially in reference to things she is passionate about. The first time I met Wilma, we talked about our time spent in the public-school system. I was a Special Education teacher and that was a common interest for both of us. Our career choices kept bringing us together. We didn't seem to be two people that would enjoy spending time together, but we did. She would say, "Girl, I have this idea and you are the perfect person to help me with it!" We would laugh and before long, Wilma would come up with an idea and off we'd go! So somewhere in our interactions with each other, a relationship started to materialize. Wilma has so much positive energy. She encourages me to keep trying new things. I love her unselfish spirit.

Wilma: I think Pennie Mae is beginning to recognize and understand all my phobias and fetishes in a way nobody else can. I don't open up to a lot of people. Since our first meeting and throughout the maturation of our friendship, it has been my hope that she knows how I feel about her. If she didn't before, hopefully she does now!

I look to her as a spiritual mentor. Along this journey, she helps me see things in another light. "It is the start that ensures a good finish," someone said. I think because we built our friendship on the right start, that solid foundation is going to serve us well until the end.

Pennie Mae: Friendship is a relationship that I don't take lightly, so I decided to look up the meaning of what it means to be a friend. A friend is a person whom one knows, likes, and trusts; and one attached to another by affection or esteem.

Friendship is a relationship of mutual affection between people. Friendship in adulthood provides companionship, affection, as well as emotional support, and contributes positively to mental well-being and improved physical health.

Friends are people who value their relationship, who have trust, mutual respect, love, and affection for one another. They provide emotional support and contribute positively to the mental well-being of each other. So, with this definition in mind, I will try to describe my friendship with Wilma and other friends that are dear to my heart.

I'm not sure when I met Wilma for the first time or when we started to consider ourselves as friends. My mind took me back to a women's retreat. We were sharing some extremely heavy testimony when Wilma stood and shared some things about her, very personal things, that I thought were amazing. One thing that touched my heart was her testimony about the passing of her first child. How could this fun, loving, carefree person have this kind of heartache stored inside? The more she talked about her experiences and how God had seen her through a very difficult time in her life, I thought it would be neat to get to know her better.

As we talked, we realized we shared similar interests. We were both teachers for many years and enjoyed working with children. We also have a passion for helping and encouraging children, more specifically, children with special needs. I worked with special needs children for over twenty years as a school teacher and enjoyed every day of my experience. I had challenging days, and a few challenging nights as I pondered ways to help them meet their educational and social needs.

Wilma and I have worked on several projects together, and it has always been a delightful experience. When we get together, we laugh, cry and talk for hours on end about so many things.

We also share a love and mutual respect for our relationship with God.

Friends are hard to come by. It is important to show others that you value their relationship. Friends don't always agree, but they don't slander each other. They have mutual respect for each other's opinion. If you're looking for true friendship, pay attention to the traits below.

ATTRIBUTES OF TRUE CHRISTIAN FRIENDS: JUST MY THOUGHTS

by Pennie Mae

A true (Christian) friend should aspire to portray the attributes of Christ. Being a true friend is hard work, and we should not tread lightly. A good (Christian) friend, should...

1-Love others as Jesus loves us

Who do you have this kind of love for? This kind of love can't be taken lightly. Jesus loves us beyond measure and He gives us a great model to emulate. We may not have to die for someone to show them we would like to be their friend, but we can start with something easy like being a good listener.

Every time we are called upon may not always be a time to give advice. Sometimes we just want someone to listen. Many times, in talking about things out loud, we can solve our own problems. True Christian friendships provide help and/or encouragement.

Philippians 2:3 (KJV) says, "Let nothing be done through strife or vain glory, but in lowliness of mind let each esteem other better than themselves.

Sometimes you must place others' needs above your own. When you do this, you may be well on your way to following the example of Jesus, and you will probably gain a true friend in the process.

2-Take friends as they are, with the good and the bad, as we see it

A friend loveth at all times, and a brother is born for adversity, (Proverbs 17:17, KJV).
Knowing someone well does not make us a "to die for" friend. Do you find that some people only stick around when things are going well? Only to disappear when you are down and in distress. Are you available when it's inconvenient and you must make a few sacrifices, or do you leave a

relationship when you are not reaping a benefit? Friends stick around even when it is not about them. They are willing to put someone else's needs above their own. Friendship means loving at all times.

3-Know that trusting completely is a process, don't give up so easily

A man that hath friends must shew himself friendly: and there is a friend that sticketh closer than a brother, (Proverbs 18:24, KJV).

We all need friends that we can count on, stay close to, and offer help when needed. As we look for a true friend in others, we must make sure we are a true friend ourselves. Pray and ask God to help you be the kind of friend that He would have you to be. If we work on ourselves first, friendship will find us. One genuine friend will certainly outweigh five that you thought were your friends.

4-Give your friends room to breathe

1 Corinthians 13:7 says, "Love always protects, always trust, always hopes, always perseveres."

Friends have mutual love and respect for each other's similarities and differences. Be aware of your history. Is it a healthy relationship? Do you each celebrate your accomplishments, or do you notice signs of jealousy? Are you in for what you can get out of the relationship, recognition, popularity? At the end of the day, can you sit back and say, "Boy, that was fun. I can't wait until the next opportunity?"

5-Praise and correction should be meaningful, not meaningless

Faithful are the wounds of a friend; but the kisses of an enemy are deceitful (Proverbs 27:6, KJV).

A friend may have to give you hard, I don't want to hear this advice at times, but they do it for your good, not to hurt you. Always consider the source. A friend will have your best interest at heart.

Do you recognize areas in your friendships that may need a little work in your efforts to build stronger friendships? Don't worry if you don't have a lot of close friends. Remember, true Christian friendships are hard to find, it takes time, it's a process. *When you find a good friend, do your part to nurture and savor your relationship through the good and difficult times and trials of life. A friend values your differences and similarities. As we grow up, we realize it is less important to have lots of friends and more important to have real ones.*

ABOUT THE AUTHORS

Brenda Johnson is a retired school teacher of 32 years. Graduated from Alcorn State University with a degree in Special Education and a masters from Mississippi Valley State University with a degree in Learning Disability. She has a love for writing and reading, and on occasion refinishes furniture. When she is not working on a project, she enjoys spending time with her family and dear friends.

Michelle Morgan Spady, Principal, B'Artful, LLC, is also an Author and Creative Entrepreneur. She matriculated from University of Utah, with a degree in English and Business. To date she has ten published books to her credit. Four of her published works are the result of co-authoring and collaborating with others. Michelle founded a 501 (c) (3) not-for-profit, The Literacy Art and Mind Foundation; focusing on the infusion of literacy, art and mindfulness. In her books she weaves themes of anti-violence, bullying, love and friendship. All of her titles can be found at

Amazon and all online retailers. Visit her online at www.michellespady.com or b-artful.com.

4

DIVINE MENTORING

YVETTE WILSON BENTLEY

What would be your biggest fear moving into a new neighborhood? Not knowing what to expect from your neighbors? Or how to learn your way around without getting lost? These questions occupied my mind when I moved into my current neighborhood.

Gone were the days of being the life of the party, the social butterfly of the neighborhood. I had matured beyond those years, thank God! My preference was to be a quiet neighbor surrounded by quiet neighbors. I like neighbors that keep to themselves, mind their own business but are friendly enough to speak and carry on an occasional casual conversation when passing.

Four years ago, I went to view a potential rental property, and the property manager introduced me to a lady name Janet. Janet had a cheerful, vibrant demeanor. She smiled and told me that she had lived there for two years and hoped I liked the unit. I found that I liked both the unit and the neighborhood and moved in two weeks later.

Janet, as it turns out, was the perfect next-door neighbor. We shared a lot in common, particularly life lessons filed under Home Training 101. Janet was big on people respecting each other's privacy and getting to know her gave me a new perspective on what that meant. I came home from work one day, and Janet's interior door was open but secured by her storm door. I took the open door as an invitation and walked up to the door. Before I could knock, Janet said, "Yvette, you're going to have to come back some other time because I am talking right now." I waved my hand and made my way back to my own unit.

I contemplated that experience for a couple of days. Janet's tone was not harsh or rude, so there was no reason for me to feel offended. Yet, I couldn't understand why that experience stayed on my mind as long as it did. On the second day, the message became clear – just because her door was open didn't mean she wanted company. Perhaps like many people during the warmer months, she was allowing the sunshine and fresh air to fill up her home. I reflected on my younger years, when I always had people running in and out of my house. Many days I came home from work, wanting to sit quietly. But that would last all of five minutes, if that. Several of my then-neighbors would see me come home from work, and by the time I'd been home ten minutes, there they were. I gave people the impression I ran an open house; anytime was a good time to knock on my door. Some days that made me angry. *Don't they know I just got home from work? Why can't they let me have a few minutes to myself before barging in on me?* Connecting my past with my present provided me the answer. I did not have any boundaries in the past. However, my present neighbor chose to exercise her boundaries. Talk about a moment of clarity. A lesson well taught is a lesson well-learned, my grandmother used to say. Janet had boundaries and had no issue enforcing her boundaries as needed.

It is okay to have boundaries and okay to

enforce them. In the past, I had allowed people to be intrusive. Janet taught me that if I stand on my principles and enforce my boundaries, I don't have to worry about intrusion nor would I allow myself to intrude on anyone else.

Unbeknownst to her, this was the beginning of Janet mentoring me. From that day on, when I knocked on her door, it was because I was invited and therefore welcomed. I was like a sponge absorbing water whenever I was in her company. I always walked away with knowledge or wisdom she imparted into me. I also walked away with tangible items – a purse, a pair of shoes, clothes, costume jewelry – "girlie" things. I tried to refuse at times, but she wouldn't hear of it.

Janet would tell me that I couldn't tell her what to do; she was doing what God put on her heart to do. Many times, I wanted to reciprocate and gift her with various things as well. If I didn't give her advance notice, this went smoothly. However, if I told her what I intended to do, she wouldn't hear of it. "I don't need you giving me anything. You are going to mess up my blessings," Janet would exclaim.

I'd tell her, "Look, the same God that blesses you blesses me too," and the biggest smile would come across her face. "Okay, sis," she'd laugh. And a few seconds later, I'd join her in the laughter. That exchange became one of the biggest running jokes of our friendship.

Dealing with people, places or situations can present its share of challenges. Things happen that make me take a step back, draw a deep breath and contemplate whether to respond or react. Most of the time, my preference is the latter. My instinct is to run on my emotions, which can lead to me becoming confrontational.

I remember being extremely frustrated with one of my other neighbors over a situation. I discussed the situation with Janet. I felt I had been violated and expressed to her how I wanted to react. As I ranted and raved, Janet remained quiet. She listened patiently and intently to everything I had to say. When I was finished, she said, "Sis, you are going to have to take the high road and walk away from that person and that situation."

"Why do I have to take the high road when they wronged me?" I inquired.

"Because, it's the right thing to do."

"Why should I take the high road when I have done nothing wrong, Janet?"

"Because as a child of God, it's the right thing

to do." Janet picked up her walking cane which was lying on the floor. She rested her hands on the top of the cane then propped her chin atop of her hands. She sighed and gave me a look. I knew she was waiting for my response, but I was silent. Reminding me that I was a child of God got my attention. Even if I wanted to argue with that, it was an argument I could not win.

As Christians, Janet explained, we must always look for the opportunity to do the right thing, even when we've been wronged. Her words and wisdom were familiar. Her point had been taught and emphasized my entire life. What grabbed my attention was Janet's delivery. Her tone was firm yet soothing to my spirit. Though she was being honest with me, the tone of her voice was not indicative of any hostility. In fact, her tone oozed love and compassion. As she continued to speak, her eyes shined bright, her smile was huge, and she appeared to have a glow. What I thought to be a regular conversation proved to be a spiritual experience.

After our time together, I went home and spent some time praying and meditating. As I sat quietly, I heard God's voice say, "Taking the high road keeps you on the road that I have paved especially for you." What a profound revelation! I have heard sermons, Sunday School lessons and countless talks from my parents, grandparents and others around the kitchen table. Until God revealed to me that the concept of taking the high road is to stay on His path for me, I merely viewed the idea as doing the right thing. I had never connected taking the high road to being beneficial. This revelation provided me with new perspective. It was also a transformational moment on my Christian journey that I will always cherish.

I was ecstatic to share my spiritual experience with Janet a few weeks later. Together, we laughed, cried and gave God praise for His revelation and what He was doing in our lives, individually and collectively. I had another revelation from God shortly thereafter. He revealed that my connection with Janet was not coincidental. God intentionally positioned me to become Janet's next-door neighbor, so He could use her to mentor and minister to me. Talking about God giving you what you need when you need it! I am so glad God's name is God and not Yvette. Had I had a hand in dictating the course of my friendship with Janet, I would have cheated myself out of what He had in store for me.

Once, Janet and I conversed about some of the neighborhood events that had taken place since I moved in. The neighbor I had the dispute with the year before was found dead from an apparent suicide. A few people moved away, and in turn, we found ourselves with several new neighbors. We even witnessed children riding their bicycles and playing with one another, which was rare. Then there was the neighboring family that proved to be a public nuisance during the eighteen months they lived on our street before their eviction. A few of us made a joke about throwing a block party. We didn't have the party, but the consensus was most of us breathed a sigh of relief once we knew they had vacated the premises. That crew was scandalous, to say the least. Janet said they would steal anything that wasn't nailed down. I laughed and added that they looked like they would steal nails and all. "Come spring, no later than summer, I won't be here," Janet told me. We talked more about her decision to move, and I discovered a few of my own reasons for contemplating a possible move.

By the time December rolled around, the trees

in the neighborhood were bare from the fallen leaves and the temperatures had stabilized in the 30s and 40s. This was typical Kentucky weather for late fall/early winter. Christmas was about two weeks away. For the first time in almost four years, I had figured out what I was going to give Janet for Christmas. Rather than calling her and announcing that I was coming over to bring her a gift, I planned to ask if I could stop by for a quick chat. Once inside her place, I would surprise her with my gift. *She won't be able to stop me or do anything about it*, I told myself. Catching her off guard had to work because all my other attempts had failed.

On Tuesday, December 19, 2017, I received a phone call from my landlord, and I was not prepared for what he would say. He advised me that Janet had passed away. *Passed away?* He said one of our other neighbors had noticed a package on Janet's porch that had been there for three days and called the police. According to the coroner, Janet had been deceased for those three days. I was devastated. I knew Janet bore her share of health challenges. However, I never thought about receiving a phone call that she had passed away.

Life is but a moment. I have seen people who

are here one minute and gone the next. When my father passed away in 2003, I was with him two hours prior to his passing. I am grateful my last moments with him were loving and positive. I had the same experience with Janet. Our last conversation, two days before she passed away, was her allowing me to vent about a situation and her telling me again to take the high road.

At her funeral, the minister said there were two things about Janet that were true. Janet loved people and she loved Jesus. As far as I was concerned, nothing else needed to be said. For those who knew and loved Janet, it was the perfect description of her life and legacy. The most profound description doesn't always require an abundance of words. It was short, sweet and to the point. I believe Janet was smiling down on us at that moment and was quite pleased with those words as she was settling into her new heavenly home.

"An experienced and trusted advisor" is how *Webster's Dictionary* defines a mentor. This is the perfect depiction of my relationship with Janet. Had I told her that she was my mentor, she would have worn me down to a pebble trying to convince me otherwise. God shows me some things that don't need to be verbalized as it will water down the richness of the experience He has designed for me. I am truly blessed to have had Janet as a neighbor, friend and mentor.

When I moved into my new neighborhood, I was worried about what to expect and learning my way around, but God had something greater in store for me. He had Janet. It's been two months since Janet went home with the Lord. And a quick glance at the calendar tells me today is her birthday. I miss her every day.

The sisterhood, friendship, fellowship and Christian love she imparted to me is priceless. It is an honor and privilege to have known Janet. She was an amazing person. And did I mention she could sing? Oh, my! She would tear the roof off with her rich and beautiful God-given voice. If Janet was here, I would say, "Janet, I thank God for you. Thank you for being such a great sister/ friend, neighbor and mentor. Yes, I said thanks for being a great mentor and guess what? There's nothing you can do about it!"

About the Author

Yvette Wilson Bentley, notable nonfiction and self-help author, has worked diligently to become a vehicle of change since 2012. Slated for launch in January 2018, S.H.E is Helpful (Self-Help Empowerment) was birthed to focus on empowering others to help themselves and then to "pass the baton" by helping others.

Yvette has been a contributing writer for newsletters and magazines as well as featured speaker, panelist and conference/summits lead facilitator. She is also an advocate and supporter for philanthropic projects and various social justice issues such as addiction and recovery, domestic violence, sexual assault and homelessness.

Visit her online at www.mynameisyvette.com

5

INFLUENTIAL MENTORS

RENEE SPIVEY

There's something to be said about having a mentor. Someone who encourages you to be your best self, to try new things and gives you good advice along the way. Someone who is interested in your success and does whatever they can to help you succeed.

During my life, I have had people that have encouraged me along the way, but the four that most stand out are Marlive Harris, Jacquelin Thomas, Stacy Hawkins Adams and Tyora Moody.

Of course, my mother was my first mentor. If not for her guidance, love and stern hand, I know

I would not be the person I am today. I am not perfect by any stretch of the imagination, but I have many redeeming qualities that I now recognize and appreciate.

My mother instilled values in me such as honesty, integrity, love and respect for others. She taught my sisters and I to always be there for each other and when we had differences, to work through them because we would always need each other. My mother taught me the value of hard work and how to push through even when I'm tired and don't feel like it. She tried to protect me from myself and others, but when I was younger, I did not appreciate it. I felt that she was too mean and did not want me to have any fun.

My mother will forever be my greatest mentor, but these four ladies have really helped me in recent years.

When I first got into the literary scene, I became a member of TheGRITS, an online book club. Marlive Harris, also known as MsGRITS, was the moderator of the group. I learned so much from her, not only from the book related info she shared in the group. When I expressed a desire to work with authors, she gave me all kinds of advice on what I needed to do. She introduced me to some authors and helped me set up face to face meetings with them. The first event I hosted via my now defunct event planning service, Stuff Happens! Event Planning, was with the legendary Francis Ray in 2005. She, along with Jacquelin Thomas and Felicia Mason had written an anthology entitled *How Sweet the Sound*. These were some of my favorite authors and with Francis being somewhat local (she was in Dallas and I'm in Huntsville), she agreed to let me host a release party for her at the Houston Public Library.

Marlive not only drove Francis from Dallas to Houston, but she helped me with every aspect of the event, including lining up local singing talent, securing the venue, etc. She also helped me craft letters to potential sponsors for the event.

When I wanted to branch out on my own and no longer write reviews for The RAWSISTAZ Reviewers (TRR), Marlive gave me instructions and advice on how to not only handle leaving TRR in the right manner, but also shared with me how to purchase a domain name, hosting, etc. I started out on Blogger, which was good for what I needed at the time. Then the web design bug hit and I wanted to branch out from Blogger and create a custom website. From Blogger, I went to

WordPress and that was a totally different animal. It was difficult to understand the coding at first and I was easily frustrated. When I became frustrated and wanted to give up, Marlive encouraged me and walked me through how to change the coding to make the site do what I wanted it to do.

If it weren't for Marlive, I wouldn't have had the moderate success I had as a literary blogger and website designer. When she decided to leave the literary industry, she gave me my first client, national bestselling author, Brenda Jackson. She handled posting Brenda's monthly newsletter on MySpace, and that job became mine, which in turn led to handling many other projects for Brenda over the course of the next nine years.

Though Marlive is no longer a part of the literary industry, her impact was long lasting and far reaching and I am grateful for the opportunity to have met her and learned at her feet.

∞

Back in 2015, national bestselling author Jacquelin Thomas, then with Brown Girl Books, offered a workshop on submitting your manuscript to publishers. On a whim, I decided to take this course because I was toying with the idea of finally writing my life story. Personally, I didn't have much hope of any publisher accepting my manuscript, but I wanted to learn what I needed to do just in case. Imagine my surprise when Jacquelin told me she loved what I had submitted and was interested in publishing it through Brown Girls Books. She instructed me to submit my query letter, outline, synopsis and the first three pages of the book to her and she would send me an official acceptance. Unfortunately, this never happened because the Jacquelin Thomas

Presents division of Brown Girls Books was dissolved as she took on more managerial roles as the COO of the company. Even though the book didn't get published through that publisher, Jacquelin still expressed interest in helping me write the book and get it published. She told me what books to purchase that would help my writing and offered lots of other advice and encouragement along the way. If it weren't for Jacquelin, my book, *Once Broken: A Journey to Restoration*, would still be a thought instead of an actual publication available for purchase.

Jacquelin has even encouraged me to try my hand at writing fiction. I've only written non-fiction. However, Jacquelin has faith that I can do it, so I believe I will try it. It may not be romance, though. If I don't go that route, I may continue writing non-fiction and aim to be the next Priscilla Shirer.

∞

Stacy Hawkins Adams is an award-winning author of several exceptional novels and is someone else that has become a valuable mentor to me. Stacy offered a writing group via Facebook, Focused Writers Membership Community and I decided to join since I was getting serious about this writing journey. There is a fee involved, but it is well worth the nominal amount I pay each month.

I've received so many good writing tips and so much encouragement from being a part of this group. The members of the group get to talk to Stacy via conference call each month and each member gets their time to shine, sharing our success and our struggles. After that, Stacy facilitates a topic discussion. For someone of Stacy's caliber to take time out of her schedule to mentor you and provide you with tools to help your literary career is a once in a lifetime opportunity that I do not take for granted.

∞

If you are interested in anything literary related and don't know Tyora Moody, you need to get to know her. Tyora is small in stature, but she's a powerhouse in the literary industry. Where Marlive left off, Tyora stepped in as far as teaching me the ins and outs of the world of books. Tyora is not only an award-winning author, she is a Jill of All Trades, wearing other hats such as publisher, online publicist and graphic designer.

I'm sure Tyora doesn't even realize I consider her a mentor, but she has helped me in many ways. From hosting authors on her site, creating graphics for me, to helping me with publishing my book, I'm in awe of Tyora! I pick her brain about a myriad of things regarding the literary industry, and she is always there with a quick response, helping me think through certain things and giving me a fresh approach or outlook on things.

Sometimes I ask questions that I think are crazy or something that I should already know, but Tyora never makes me feel like my questions are dumb. Her quiet, gentle spirit is amazing.

If it were not for Tyora, I couldn't count published author as one of my achievements. Tyora read a blog post I had written about a certain dark period of my life. When she decided to put together *When Women Become Business Owners*, she graciously offered me an opportunity to contribute to the anthology. From there, I decided to expand the story and tell more than what I had originally included on the post and in the anthology. It was, and still is, a scary journey because I do not know what is around the corner. But with Ty's help, the journey is much easier.

∞

Each of my mentors saw something in me, oftentimes things I didn't see myself. Little by little, they helped me shed my insecurities and embrace life to the fullest. Each of these ladies have helped shape me into the budding literary professional I want to be. The lessons I have learned from them have also carried over into my latest and greatest venture, Women of Worth Ministries, Inc. Women of Worth Ministries, Inc., a faith-based organization located in Huntsville, Texas, seeks to enhance the lives of formerly incarcerated and homeless women within the community, or any woman desiring to increase her skillset by providing counseling, essential life, personal, work related and educational skills.

The ministry is still in its infancy stages and

we have encountered a few roadblocks, but that is not deterring us from our mission to be a light in this dark world. Thanks to some donations from both individuals and corporations, we have been able to help people locally, as well as victims of Hurricane Harvey which hit the Houston area in August 2017. We were able to take our ministry on the road last year as workshop presenters at the Christian Book Lover's Retreat and have been blessed with the opportunity again this year. We have also participated in backpack drives, toy drives for a Head Start facility and provided free hair care services to young women for their first day back to school and formal dances.

We also are in the process of planning a community wide meal for anyone who needs it. It will be held in conjunction with my church, Huntsville Church of Christ annual clothing giveaway. Once the families get the clothes they want, they can stop by the fellowship hall and pick up a free meal with no strings attached. Most places have events such as this during Thanksgiving and Christmas, but people are hungry year-round so we decided to do something different.

Other plans the ministry has is to have gently

used clothing available for women who need something suitable to wear to an interview, similar to Dress for Success, as well as provide some of the basic necessities free of charge to the women who will pass through our doors.

It is important for us to give back because we have been blessed. Having been to prison, I know firsthand the struggles ex-offenders face. The constant judgment, discrimination, and the lack of job opportunities are discouraging.

I have always known I am a nurturer, but I did not know how I would help on a grand scale. After my release from prison, I discovered there weren't many places that offered substantial help to people who are no longer incarcerated. Sure, there are halfway houses, but they don't provide aftercare services. Most organizations that have prison ministries focus primarily on preaching to inmates while they are in prison, which is excellent. But unless something is offered to help once they come home, the revolving door cycle seems to continue.

All the knowledge I have gained from my mentors, I plan to pass on to others. While my ministry is not literary related, I can still apply the things I have learned over the course of my life.

Thanks, in part, to my mentors. I am grateful they came into my life at the time they did and poured into me what they did. I did not know my life would take the path it did, but God knew and allowed me to meet these women at the appropriate time. I am thankful that Tyora, Marlive, Stacy and Jacquelin are strong black women that care not only about my journey into the literary world but many others as well. They have graciously endured countless questions from me about anything and everything, prayed with me and for me and offered sound advice and constructive criticism that I will hold in high esteem for the rest of my life.

It is important to reach back and help those in need, and it's not always about financial support either. Helping comes in many other forms and sometimes those forms offer a greater reward than a temporary monetary fix. If you ever get the opportunity, become a mentor to someone. Not only will the mentee gain knowledge and understanding, so will you. There is no greater feeling than knowing you helped make a difference in someone's life. I hope one day I will be able to pass on the knowledge I have gained to someone else and that they will pass it on, extending throughout several generations.

ABOUT THE AUTHOR

Renee Spivey is an avid reader and newly published author, is a native of Huntsville, Texas. Renee holds an Associate of Arts degree in Information Technology and is pursuing a Bachelor's degree in Business Administration from Sam Houston State University.

Renee is also the co-founder of We Are Women of Worth Ministries, Inc., a 501(c)3 non-profit organization whose main focus is to inspire, inform and encourage women from all walks of life to step out of the shadows of their past into a brighter future by offering life, personal and educational skills, to name a few.

6

FROM MANAGER TO MENTOR

MADLYN MARSHALL

In 1995, long before GRACE Ministry, Beth, as I've called her since we met, hired me for a position in her department. I had been in Georgia only a few days before I got the job. I was not a Christian when I met Beth, nor was I interested in becoming one. But I came to know her as a kind-hearted generous person. On many occasions she and several of my coworkers invited me to attend their church, and not being the least bit interested at that time, I adamantly refused their offers.

God had a different plan for my life. When I

found myself in a situation where I couldn't go any further, one of those 'nice' Christian coworkers, Esther, offered to pray for me and asked me if I knew Jesus. I told her I knew who He was, and she asked if I'd asked Him for help. I hadn't, but when I did, my life changed overnight.

After I had a few bible studies under my belt, I came to think fondly of Esther as my "Paul" and I her "Timothy". A friendship was formed, in which I was mentored, counselled, and held accountable as a new believer. That original conversation started my spiritual journey and led me to Central Baptist Church where Elizabeth Copeland, Beth, was the leader over Administration. Almost immediately, I began volunteering in the finance office and soon became the finance manager and ultimately, the CFO. By that time, Beth started her own leadership training ministry, God's People Ministry. Using principles from the book of Nehemiah and her first book, *How to Lead People Without Losing Your Mind*, Beth trained leaders in both secular and corporate environments.

When I felt prompted to start a nonprofit and name it G.R.A.C.E. Financial Ministries, Inc., I had no idea what to do or how to do it. Over the years, I'd bounced many ideas around in my head.

I wrote business concepts, ministry ideas, marketing ideas and possibilities, but the actual basis for the nonprofit was birthed, first, out of me putting my faith in Jesus Christ and then being the chief financial officer (CFO) for my local church. In my role as finance manager, I often assisted with new member's classes and taught about tithing. I enjoyed teaching bible studies that centered around tithing and being a good steward of all that God has given. I developed some of my own curriculum that was inspired by a guest speaker who attended our church.

During my time at CBC, I was mentored by an awesome man of God who I lovingly refer to as "Poppy". When I first met Pastor Ervin Arthur Kimble, known as PK to most of the congregation, he was in the pulpit delivering a message I was sure was meant just for me. At that time, PK pulled membership reports and financial reports using an old Disk Operating System, more commonly known as DOS. Over the next thirteen years, I not only earned his confidence in my ability, I believe I earned the respect of the members.

Because of my fondness for Pastor Kimble, I became very close with his wife, Jackie. During those years, Jackie demonstrated a capacity to love that scared me. She has a mother's heart and her compassion for the lost is fueled by her sincere desire for everyone to know the love of Christ. Jackie can tell when you need a hug or just need to talk. We've spent many three and four-hour lunches or dinners just talking. She's a big sister, mother figure, and a friend, all rolled up into one person. Jackie's gentle smile and reassuring words will compel you to tell her all that's troubling you, and she listens but never judges or condemns. She just loves you unconditionally and encourages you, all while helping you identify a solution to your problem, which always starts with the Word of God.

Jackie has an uncanny knack for knowing when you need to know you're not alone. A prime example of this was when my mother died. Jackie, a retired flight attendant, can fly anywhere United Airlines flies. She could be in Chicago one day and Australia the next, which she has done. When my mother died, I went home for her funeral. I was in my hotel room when I received a call from Jackie who said she was checking on me to see how I was. Five minutes later, there was a knock on the door, and it was Jackie. She'd come to be with me during that time in my life.

Fast forward several years to 2013, and a chance meeting with my former manager and ministry leader, Beth and an invitation to talk about my vision for GRACE Ministry. Elizabeth Copeland, founder of God's People Ministry had also founded Georgia Christian Business Network (GCBN), a groundbreaking resource for Christian business owners and Christian employees of corporations to network and share best practices for "Putting God Back into Business", Beth's signature tagline. Being a part of this network is a wonderful resource for learning, growing and interacting with fellow Christian professionals. Beth also offers one on one business coaching.

Over the course of several one on one coaching sessions with Beth, I was able to get a sense of how God wanted me to serve Him. Beth helped me make sense of my chaotic thoughts. I had a lot of ideas and various directions for where I thought GRACE should go. I'd done what I knew to do, but Beth helped me hone in on the specifics of what I wanted GRACE to accomplish within my community and beyond. Working with Beth and having her support has been a blessing over the years. She is one of my best champions and holds me accountable to being true to what God called me to do. Because of Beth, I have published two books: a fiction, *ReUnited A Gift from God*, and a nonfiction, *Whose Money Is It?* Beth challenges me and pushes me to be all that God has called me to be. She is relentless and holds me accountable to the vision God has given me for GRACE. Beth also knows when I need prayer and an encouraging word. I've gotten texts from her in the wee hours of the morning saying, "I was thinking about you and I'm praying for you."

Working with Beth and GCBN, I have had the opportunity to facilitate financial budgeting workshops, attend several women's conferences that allowed me to meet and interact with other strong godly women who are professional business and community leaders. It was at such a conference where I met another godly woman who introduced me to Tyora Moody when I was looking for someone to do my book cover and edits. If you have an opportunity to attend a GCBN networking event, a lunch and learn or a conference, you will hear Beth say, "*God has a plan (Jeremiah 29:11)...*" to which you will respond, "*and I'm a part of it.*"

The experience and confidence I've gained from my coaching sessions and workshops empowered me to stretch beyond my comfort zone. Along the way, I met another awesome woman of God, whose compassion and life story is awe inspiring. Dr. Gayle Daniels is the founder of Words of Comfort Ministries Inc., (WOC) located in Snellville, GA. I began my association with Dr. Daniels by serving as a volunteer. I've watched Dr. Daniels and her close friends and board members for several years, and I've never experienced such a close, loving and caring relationship as these ladies share. There was no infighting, jealousy or cat fighting that one would assume happens when five strong willed women get together. Instead, I saw a sincere love for one another. When they disagree, it is done with respect and understanding. These women share each other's burdens, pray for one another and hold each other accountable. It's inspiring, so inspiring that when asked to become a board member, I was honored and gladly accepted.

Through my partnership and service with WOC, I've learned women can work and play together, laugh and have fun while glorifying God. The relationships I've had the joy of experiencing have been a blessing to me in more ways than one. I learned that sometimes you must come out of your comfort zone and take a chance on meeting people. Women oftentimes are accused of being catty or backstabbers. Some believe women's relationships are like what is depicted on reality TV: infighting, suspicious, mistrusting, constantly accusing one another of some offense. What I say to those individuals is stop watching reality TV and start developing positive godly relationships with positive godly women.

I've had some hurtful relationships along the way. But, I also learned a lot from those relationships. I've learned the dynamics of relationships. Not everyone is meant to be a lifetime friend, some are only for a season and some are only for a reason. Knowing the difference has saved me a lot of hurt. The relationships that didn't go as I thought they should was not because of the individuals. Once I understood the dynamics and saw the reason or realized the season, I could remember each one with fondness and feel no regrets. Now, opening myself up to other awesome interactions with mighty women of God becomes an exciting adventure.

If it hadn't been for Beth and her sincere kindness, I wouldn't have been exposed to these examples of godly women. The three dynamic ladies I've discussed here all love the Lord with all their hearts and with all their minds. They are devoted to showing and sharing the love of Christ. They challenged me to grow spiritually and to be a better person, inside and out. Because of them, I am a much better woman, friend, and Christian leader.

ABOUT THE AUTHOR

Madlyn Marshall is the Founder of G.R.A.C.E. Financial Ministry, Inc. G.R.A.C.E. is an acronym for "God's Resources Advancing Christian Evangelism". G.R.A.C.E. Financial Ministry provides debt counseling, money management, along with the tools for credit restoration using biblical principles. Madlyn has a heart for outreach, serving the community and actively works with non-profit organizations that assist individuals who are temporarily displaced and suffering hardships due to unemployment or underemployed.

Madlyn is an author of several short stories and poems published under her own company, G.R.A.C.E. Publishing Inc. The publishing company was established to publish biblical studies, focused on money management, and fictional inspirational writing.

Madlyn also volunteers her years of experience to help other organizations such as Every Woman Works, by facilitating financial education workshops for the women in the program as they re-enter the job market. She also conducts budgeting workshops for the residents at the Nicholas House a residential shelter located in downtown Atlanta to equip the residents there to prepare to re-entry to living on their own and avoid the pitfalls that may have caused their financial crisis situation.

PART II

HOW TO MAKE MEANINGFUL CONNECTIONS

7

NAVIGATING THE SEASONS OF FRIENDSHIPS

TYORA MOODY

As I draw closer to turning fifty years old, I often find myself reflecting on the number of friends I have had over the years. Friends come and go, but I firmly believe friendships are for a purpose and season of your life. Some people are blessed enough to have friends that are with them through many seasons of their lives, while others like me, have friends for particular seasons.

My memories of friendships past are wrapped around significant periods of my life. These periods of life include starting new schools, college years, single years, married life and my life now.

Ecclesiastes 3:1 states, "There is a time for everything, and a season for every activity under the heavens." I encourage you to take a walk back with me through your life as you read this chapter. Feel free to grab your journal and jot down your personal timeline. I have provided questions along the way. Your timeline may not resemble mine, but you will probably have your own significant time periods when your friendships shifted.

THE SCHOOL YEARS

My mom has a friend who she's been friends with since third grade. Both of them are in their late sixties now, and I am always astounded with how she has remained friends with a person her whole life who is not family.

I am not in touch with many of my friends from elementary, middle or high school, but many of the memories remain with me. I had three major seasons of friendships during my school years.

New school after 4th grade: Fourth grade was a particular interesting time. I had friends that were not a good influence on me. My fourth-grade teacher, Mrs. Jones, noticed this too and proceeded to let my parents know. My parents switched me from public school to Catholic school in fifth grade, and this was a pretty drastic change for me. It was first time I found myself adjusting to a new school environment, cut-off from previous friends.

Move in the middle of 8th grade: My parents moved from New York to South Carolina in the middle of my eighth grade year. This move was perhaps the most significant because I never quite fit in and remembered I couldn't wait to graduate high school. What is interesting is some of the first friends I made when I moved to the South are still the ones I remain in contact with, though mainly through social media.

College Years: I had a group of roommates and friends that I hung out with, but my roommate from my last two years in college is the main person I keep contact with. We reach out periodically via social media and email. I remember trying to keep in touch with former classmates with letters and cards (this was before the ascent of email). After marked periods of not receiving any communication back, you realize the friendships had dissolved and were for a period of time.

- *Do you still have contact with a friend or friends from elementary school? How do you remain in contact?*
- *Do you still have contact with a friend or friends from middle school? How do you remain in contact?*
- *Do you still have contact with a friend or friends from high school? How do you remain in contact?*
- *Do you still have contact with a friend or friends from college? How do you remain in contact?*

THE ADULT YEARS

There is such a difference in life at age twenty as compared to age forty. I recently reached the twentieth anniversary of being at my job. I started my career single, got married and in the past decade returned to being single again. My relationship status in many ways defined my friends. During my twenties, the majority of the woman I hung around were single like me.

When I got married in 2000, I hung out with other married women who were also part of the Air Force community on base. I became pretty involved teaching Sunday School and participating in bible study on base. When my husband deployed, I found a source of support amongst the other Air Force wives who understood what it was like to be lonely at home, wondering what was happening overseas.

I always had some awkwardness around other women when the topic of children came up because I wasn't a mother, but the one thing I had in common ended in 2009, when my divorce was finalized. This was one of those times in my life when I consciously moved on because that wasn't a community I could remain a part of and I needed to move forward.

- *Are you currently single, married, divorced or widowed?*
- *Do you find your relationship status defines your friendships?*
- *If you're single and around married friends, what are your experiences?*
- *Have you been recently divorced? Did you find your friendships shifted?*

- *Did you enlist in the military or live on a
  military installation? Do you still keep up with
  friends?*

THE DEEPER CONNECTIONS

My dearest and deepest friendships are mainly
with people I've known an incredible long time
(some of them my entire life) and who I have
consistent face-to-face contact. My mom and
sister are the ones I refer to as my BFF's (best
friends forever), but I also have a close relationship
with co-workers I've known for twenty years of
sharing the same workspaces. We have all grown
older and shared the crazy ups and downs of being
in state government jobs, and we don't mind
sharing our lives outside of work. It's good to take
time out of your daily grind to vent, but also let
others know you're praying for them.

- *Who do you currently have your deepest
  friendships with?*
- *How long have you been friends?*
- *What keeps your friendship strong?*

RECONNECTING WITH PAST FRIENDSHIPS

With the many people I've called friends, I can't say that I had friendships that were toxic in anyway. My past friendships were with really good people who for whatever reason, usually timing, locations, changes in life, we all grew apart. I fondly remember events and people and count it all joy to have those connections at those particular times in my life. On occasion, I think it would be great to figure out where people are now.

Facebook boasts over two billion active users which is probably why it remains the number one social media platform. Their term "friends" may be a bit shaky, but finding old friends starts with a search. If your past friends have websites or other social media profiles, Google is great for these types of searches. Talking to old classmates or other mutual friends may also help further your search for an old friend. Depending on how determined you are, I've known people who've had great success finding old friends with websites like Classmate.com.

You may find it a treat to connect with a friend from the past, if it's only to check-in with their life now. If you're close in proximity, the timing may be right to rekindle the connection. Just keep in mind that people change and may not always be open.

- *Is there someone you want to reconnect with from the past?*
- *Have you used any searches to find and locate past friends?*
- *What caused you to lose contact with some of your past friends?*

7 WAYS TO EXPLORE NEW FRIENDSHIPS

In my timeline, there were several times where I was left finding new friends. Maybe you're at a time in your life where you want to explore new friendships. Here are a few ways to find new friendships.

1. **If you're starting a new job,** introduce yourself. Ask others if they want to go out for lunch. Likewise, if there are new people starting where you work, make them feel welcome. Be careful and cautious not to use the time to get into work gossip.

2. If you're attending a new church, don't become a "pew sitter." Get involved by attending Sunday School or bible study. If you have the pipes, consider joining the choir. Volunteer at events and offer your help in the kitchen.

3. Are you a mom? Do you have children in school? Participate in the local PTA's and volunteer your time to get to know other parents.

4. What types of hobbies do you enjoy? Check out Meetup.com to see if there are local events or groups in your area. Whether you crotchet, play basketball, enjoy hiking, etc., you will likely find people with similar interests.

5. If you're single, check out local single events. Meetups also works for relationships too.

6. Are you an avid reader? Search for local book clubs in your area. Consider searching Google, Facebook or Twitter to find out more about book clubs. They often share their book of the month. Don't forget to get a library card from your public library. Sometimes book clubs meet at the library.

7. You can't beat social media for connections.

Facebook does provide a variety of ways to meet people via groups. Probably the deeper connections are made if you have conversations off the platform via phone or face-to-face if possible.

Happy friend-hunting to you. Be open-minded and be yourself. Understand everyone is not meant to be a deep close friend. With many people living longer, loneliness is becoming a major health factor. Learning to keep connections and make new connections will go a long way towards your health too.

ABOUT THE AUTHOR

Tyora Moody is the author of Soul-Searching Suspense books which include the Reed Family Series, Eugeena Patterson Mysteries, Serena Manchester Series, and the Victory Gospel Series. She is also the author of The Literary Entrepreneur Series, editor for the Stepping Into Victory Compilations and Aspiring Love Short Stories Compilations under her company, Tymm Publishing LLC.

As a literary-focused entrepreneur, she has assisted countless authors with developing an online presence via her design and marketing company, Tywebbin Creations LLC. Popular services include book covers, book formatting, and book trailers.

To contact Tyora about book club discussions or for book marketing workshops, visit her online at TyoraMoody.com.

8

CREATING THE TRIBE

JEANETTE HILL

The reason there are so many clichés and adages about villages and tribes is because it is true. No one makes it on their own. By the same token, no one can fill all the roles we need to become better women, mothers, wives, friends or people.

I have had a tribe of women warriors throughout my life. The members have changed over the years, hopefully, because I have changed...for the better.

Interestingly enough, I did not consciously seek these women out. Several I didn't think I needed and a few...I didn't want. Since I don't have a lot of faith in coincidences, I can only attribute these relationships to God knowing what I needed better than I did.

Often when we think of friendship, we think of good times, encouragement and similar lifestyles as being the most impactful in our lives. While this is often the case, I have been blessed with friends who in other areas would be considered mentors of a sort. Women who 'call you on your mess' as the saying goes.

I am going to acknowledge my tribe in quadrants. Women who have impacted my life in ways none of us may have intended but have made me a better woman and hopefully, I have had a similar impact on their lives.

THE ENCOURAGER

Joan was my first encourager after my mother. In spite of being ignored and insulted, she stood by a frightened, angry pregnant teenager. I had lost my scholarships, the respect of those I admired and was told by the baby's father and his mother to get an abortion because they wanted no part of the baby's life. I decided I would go into isolation, but it didn't bother her. She and her boyfriend

Dave would come to my house and knock on the door until I opened it—sometimes waiting fifteen to twenty minutes for me to respond. She would sit with me for several hours attempting to converse even though I wouldn't speak. After a while, she would get up, tell me that everything was going to be alright. With a hug, she would tell me she loved me and leave as tears slowly worked their way down my face.

Every now and then, I would call Sally Joan and sit on the phone for several hours saying no more than the initial hello. I was at a loss to explain how I felt. But every so often, she would whisper, "It's okay," until I managed to say I needed to go. She didn't share with me that she was pregnant as well and was having complications with her pregnancy. She lost her baby shortly after I delivered mine. I was so wrapped up in my own dilemma that I didn't know what to say to her. As I stuttered to find words of comfort, she told me to get ready, she was coming to take me shopping for baby clothes.

Though we don't see or even talk to each other for years at a time, when we do get together, it's as though no time has passed. And even though we are both grandmothers now, she is still very much my encourager—pumping me up on Facebook, sending her annual updates and asking how the 'girls' are doing and passing along her love.

THE WARRIORS

Just living brings drama and chaos. There is no avoiding it, and I think I've had more than my share. Some naturally...and some self-inflicted. During those midnight hour experiences, there were people like Sandra as most of us called her. She grew up in a situation that statisticians wouldn't even have given her odds for, so fighting to survive was not anything new for her. To look at her, you wouldn't think it but once she got that 'look', there was no doubt it was on. Though she didn't want a career, I did. And when she discovered how serious I was about the pursuit, she pushed me like she was getting a part of my paycheck. We helped each other raise our children and in spite of the craziness that divorce brings, our kids have turned out pretty good.

I had church and corporate warriors, who wouldn't let anyone finish a sentence that cast me in a negative light. My strong prayer warrior sisters, like Nona would not only confront my attacker but mount a charge against the gates of hell on my behalf and stop me from thinking, saying or acting as if I was anything less than a child of the most high God. She would get in my face and refuse to let me listen to the lies of the enemy. When I chose to fight, she wouldn't let me fight alone. She was definitely the Okoye to my T'challa. She made me understand that if there was going to be a fight, I wanted the fighters with me.

SERGEANT-AT-ARMS

We all need this woman. The friend who has no problem calling you on your mess. Reaffirming that I knew I was better than my current situation and it was time I walked and behaved like it. For me, that person was Allie Johnson. Allie was old enough to be my mother but she fit in with all ages. At almost six feet tall, her soft voice and quiet nature belied the tower of strength and wisdom she possessed. Though she could have passed for Caucasian without question, which in East Texas would have been a blessing, she took every opportunity to let anyone know she was African American and proud of it. Allie and I worked together for a number of years for the federal government. After being overlooked for a promotion again, I reached a crucial turning point in my career and decided I would give up and do like other employees—arrive to work late, take long lunches, and do just enough to get by. It seemed to work for others, why not me?

Allie waited until the two of us were alone sorting through old files in the back and told me doing what everybody else was doing wouldn't work for me. She said I would have a hard time because it wasn't my character and that you never allow any person or situation diminish your character. For most African Americans, she said, character was all we had.

I tried to get her to apply for promotions but she said she was content to work where she was until she was eligible for retirement. Allie and I maintained a close personal relationship even after I went on to receive several promotions which transferred me out of that department.

THE BUDDY

We all need to live balanced lives. Achieving success must be balanced with down time, and

Marie was my down time buddy. She was, and still is, the friend I call at 4 a.m. just to talk. Between the two us, we redefined 'keeping it real.' Those times when I made a mess of my life and wanted to run away and start anew, she'd remind me that if I didn't learn the lesson from what happened, not to unpack my bags because I'd be moving again. My buddy Margaret and I have been through all phases of life together—births, deaths, divorce, illness. But none of it has changed our relationship. We go from deep-soul diving conversations that we could never share with anyone else to talking about ways to alter the price tag on a dress we said we bought on sale.

Even now, no matter how dark it looks, she always finds a positive spin to put on the situation. Then she has a drink of wine for me (I don't drink) to seal the deal.

My relationship with each of these women and a few others allowed me to grow and learn to love and accept who I am while teaching me to value them. It is important that we all have these types of women in our lives: an encourager, a warrior, a sergeant at arms, and a buddy to take us from an acorn to an oak.

The essence of what these women poured into

the different quadrants of my life, those things that mold me into the Jeanette you see, are what happens when women really connect.

ABOUT THE AUTHOR

Jeanette W. Hill is the founder and executive director of JWHill Productions, a theatrical production company and Sight Ain't Seeing Productions, a 501(C) 3, a creative arts organization that serves under-represented and under-served communities.

Hill advises her consultancy clients to write like a winner: Diligently, daringly and with every fiber of their beings. Play-writing is a business and if anyone understands the business of play-writing and production it is Jeanette Hill.

The award-winning playwright (*The Best Lesson, Dealing with Daddy's Devils* and *The Silent City*) seamlessly combines the best of traditional with urban theater. From a business perspective, Hill is a firm believer that art does not have to bow down to profit or lack of quality to be entertaining.

Jeanette Hill was featured in the documentary, "Black and Write," and selected to participate in the D.C. Black Theatre Festival. She is the 2013 recipient of the Kingdomwood Christian Film Festival's "People's Choice Award for a Stage

Play," and the winner of the renowned Atlanta Black Theatre Festival's "Best Staged Reading" award. And she is a winner of the 2014 Black Pearls Magazine Literary Excellence Awards.

Hill's community activism is demonstrated in the projects she's taken on such as anti-bullying campaigns as well as faith-based initiatives to promote the arts. She is a sought-after workshop facilitator, speaker and conference panelist.

The Akron, Ohio native currently works and resides with her family in Austin, Texas

9

FUNDAMENTAL TECHNIQUES FOR NETWORKING

DAWN MCCOY

Women have amazing opportunities to connect through ever-changing communication channels. This is true for both traditional in-person networking and social media networking.

With multiple ways of communicating, what are some networking tools to keep in mind and why? How can women position themselves to be future-proof and remain relevant with their networking strategies? This chapter reinforces fundamental techniques for women professionals to leverage resources and exponentially expand their networking focus. Additionally, networking through non-traditional and social media platforms will be explored and addressed.

Networking is more than "schmoozing" or a tool for those climbing the proverbial career ladder. Networking is the exchange of ideas where people share and teach technical concepts and connect yielding further insight. It might be summed up as goal-oriented small talk and is characterized by determining who you can be of assistance to you and vice versa.

In *Dig Your Well Before You're Thirsty*, author Harvey Mackay says, "A network is an organized collection of your personal contacts and your personal contacts' own network. Networking is finding fast how to get what you need in any given situation and helping others do the same."

In life and business, we continually build relationships. Along the way, you make new acquaintances and meet people. The most significant forums for networking happen in professional circles at meetings, conferences, or networking events. These relationships can create ties and bonds between you and others.

Why bother creating these ties? Because your network can open doors and grant access to resources you otherwise would not have at your fingertips. For instance, your network can help answer your questions. Or they can help you find the connections for a special project or growth opportunity. Your network can also help you as you advance in the field by recommending you for positions in association leadership or alerting you to opportunities as they arise. Likewise, your network can help you find volunteer opportunities related to your expertise, including serving on committees.

Tips to remember about building your networking ties:

- Reach out to new contacts and build industry connections to expand possible networks

- Use innovative technology, such as personal digital assistants (PDAs) and tablets and handheld devices to maintain contacts

- Leverage resourceful apps and technology programs

- Balance use of traditional and client relationship management tools

- Discover resources and ideas through your acquaintances

- Establish trust and connection between people on issues of mutual interest

- Expand your circle of contacts as roles and rules change

Meeting and Conference Preparation

Conferences and meetings offer endless possibilities for networking with professionals who share your interests. I have found my conference networking skills are essential to maximizing contacts in a limited timeframe. I learned that sharing my experience can also help my personal development and organizational objectives while I help others.

Developing a strategic networking plan is

simply good business that will cultivate organizational and personal growth. Motivational speaker, author and network expert George C. Fraser points out the importance of a "networking street map" for determining how to accomplish your goals.

READY, SET, NETWORK!

Once you are at the conference, keep your personal and professional goals in mind to guide your efforts. With business cards in hand, along with your preplanning and a solid and concise self-introduction in mind, jump in and start meeting people. Note the circumstances of your meetings throughout the conference in a notebook or on the reverse side of each business card you receive. This will serve as an informal way to recall your new contacts later when you follow up. Be aware that brief, but valuable conversations in a limited time frame might bring you multiple and new perspectives.

Sometimes your plan might be side-tracked by unavoidable scheduling conflicts. Be prepared to reprioritize accordingly. Likewise, it is important to pace yourself, rest, and be flexible. Unlike a regular office day, twelve-hour conference days may include both early breakfast meetings and late evening receptions.

In addition, take advantage of unplanned opportunities to build relationships throughout the conference. Watch for chances to meet seasoned professionals and keynote speakers to glean helpful support by being a "shadow" with peers. Maximize every opportunity to meet people, and you will notice the ease at which connections seem to happen. Also, sit with people you do not know at sessions and meal events to make new acquaintances.

Remember to ask questions and learn what you can about the people you meet. People enjoy talking about who they are and what they do. A few simple questions and a genuine interest will generally yield a great deal of information from anyone you meet.

CONFERENCE FOLLOW UP

Cultivating new connections is essential to ensure your efforts bring forth contacts and networks. Maintaining contacts is vital to opening doors for a mutually beneficial exchange of information.

Sometimes, as we wrestle with daily competing priorities, conference contacts and business cards sit on desks tossed aside after returning to the office. After any conference, it is critical to categorize and manage your new contacts and business cards in an electronic database or even an old-fashioned card file. Technology can simplify this effort with card scanning machines, personal digital assistants (PDAs), client relationship management apps, and other electronic capabilities. But, we must take the time to do this.

Set aside time on your calendar to contact your new acquaintances. This means carving out time in your schedule for post-conference follow up such as handwritten notes, sending email messages, and making telephone calls. If you are setting up time to meet or talk via telephone, be timely in your contacts. I sometimes send follow up notes with new articles on topics of mutual interest. Everyone has a unique personal style, time, and approach to reaching out. After just a few contacts, you will likely find what best suits you.

Implementing A Networking Plan

These seven ways to effectively implement a networking strategy will catapult you into the next level of shared, mutually-beneficial experiences with networking and development:

Review conference and meeting programs before you attend. Get familiar with the website, organizational leadership, committees, and sessions of interest. If a list of conference attendees is provided beforehand, be sure to review and highlight names of people you want to meet and prioritize making those contacts.

If you are a new attendee or the subject matter is new for you, then you might explore a "beginner track" to become better acquainted. Many meetings provide a "first-time" attendees reception or gathering that you should try to attend.

If you are a supervisor or seasoned veteran in your field, consider using conference networking to introduce members of your staff to each other and new contacts as well. These activities will bring a reasonable return on investment.

Come prepared to network. Have a supply of business cards on hand, a networking strategy, and an electronic or manual data tracking system.

Develop a concise self-introduction that explains who you are, what you do, and what value or services you share.

Set reasonable networking goals for connecting with existing colleagues and meeting new ones at conference receptions, meal functions, and in the trade show exhibit area.

Coordinate with your office colleagues beforehand about sharing responsibilities to attend overlapping functions and conference sessions. Preplanned brainstorming and business lunches are focused ways to reconnect and develop relationships at a conference. In my career, these preplanned meetings reinforced my relationships while supporting my personal knowledge and my organization's goals.

Social Media Networking

Given the shifting dynamics with social media platforms, networking has become even more important in this venue. This includes Twitter, Facebook, LinkedIn, Reddit, Instagram, YouTube, Periscope, SnapChat, and many others. One way to stay connected on these platforms is by maintaining a consistent presence. In other words, stay actively engaged by posting questions, engaging in discussions and staying present. It is helpful to do this on several platforms, ensuring variation in your posted communication, and maintaining a brand focus or message when communicating.

Most social networking platforms allow for a direct communication method through instant messaging or direct messaging to communicate with others. Through this style of informal networking, you can maintain a rapport, initiate correspondence, and cultivate friendships and professional ties. This is a viable platform to keep ongoing dialogue about issues of mutual interest.

Also, it is important to explore group networking through social media in order to expand your network. This has expanded and diversified social media communication. For instance, through LinkedIn, you can stay connected with your network and also connect with specialty groups of mutual or desired interests. In this way, you can make a point to get connected with overlapping networks and additional resources.

Some social media networking rules to keep in mind:

Know the rules of each platform, group, or forum. These can vary and include specific parameters for the type of questions or comments posted.

Know the group etiquette. Posting on Twitter is different than posting on Instagram or Facebook and daring to overlook the unspoken can be a deal-breaker if you are trying to manage viable networking.

Study the platform history. Be sure to know the protocol and background for discussions. For instance, communication on LinkedIn varies and is more professional unlike Facebook or Instagram that can include more "social" posts about personal interests.

Have clear communication. When you share a message, content, or idea, be definitive in your word usage and messaging. Using jargon or slang will not clearly communicate a message to others and might lead to confusion or misunderstanding of your intended message.

Balance direct and social communication. If you are intending to connect with someone one on one, then be sure to explore how to appropriately take the conversation offline to a direct message, telephone call, or email.

Send notes of gratitude and/or congratulations. Be sure to send along a congratulatory note or message of thanks when appropriate. This will be short but meaningful to the recipient and while succinct, the intended message can have long-lasting and memorable effects.

Make mindful self-introductions. If you are posting in a group for the first time, share a meaningful but brief self-introduction. When sending a message to another individual via direct message, be short and include one or two sentences with your specific request for the introduction. More importantly, consider using the latest video technology to do a brief, thirty-second or less self-introduction. Be sure to include your email address, social media handle, or website where people can connect with you.

Be a mentor. Support others who are learning about how to manage social media platforms. In turn, others will do the same for you with new and varied platforms such as system upgrades and new guidelines.

Take breaks regularly. It is important to continue networking but take appropriate breaks from social media. For instance, take time away from your computer two or three times per week and manage your network. You might also consider other communication methods during a break from social media such as telephone calls, emails, or handwritten notes. This variation will also make your presence and communication style memorable.

Get training. Since there are always new social media platforms, be sure to stay connected and get training about the latest trends. Doing so will ensure that you have an awareness of cutting-edge resources, tools and insights. For instance, livestream and implementation through video is trending. Get educated about how to ensure you are current with your skills and applicable networking strategies.

WOMEN NETWORKING IN THE 21ST CENTURY AND BEYOND

With shifting landscapes, women professionals must be more mindful and strategic about networking. There must be an attention to timing, pace, and the approach to social media and traditional networking. Conferences and traditional forums continue to have their appropriate place and must be balanced effectively. When women use their traditional and more sophisticated relationship management tools, they are better positioned to be more resourceful.

NETWORKING PRIORITY AND SUCCESS

Successful networking occurs when you stay connected, sustain a rapport with colleagues, and maximize your ties at conferences and other venues. Staying focused on your personal and professional goals will underscore mutual interests and expand your expertise in serving as a mentor to peers and newcomers.

Futurist John Naisbitt, author of Megatrends, summed up how important networking is when he said, "Today, we live in a world of overlapping networks, not just a constellation of networks, but a galaxy of network constellations." What a tremendous consideration to ensure that our industry explores all the possibilities to stay connected. Ask yourself the question: Is your net working?

ABOUT THE AUTHOR

Dawn McCoy is a speaker and author of *Leadership Building Blocks: An Insider's Guide to Success*. As a leadership strategist, she provides strategic services for public and private sector clients as the founder of Flourish Leadership Group, LLC, a leadership development and communications firm. Dawn is a former non-profit executive, elected Sacramento School Board trustee, and a gubernatorial board appointee. Dawn serves on national boards for families with disabilities and she received national and regional community service awards. Dawn holds a bachelor's degree from Howard University, a master's degree from Georgetown University, and certification from the Connective Leadership Institute.

www.flourishleadership.com

10

BUSINESS NETWORKING ADVICE FOR INTROVERTS

LINDA L. HARGROVE

DISCLAIMER: Portions of this article appear in my eBook, "Your Fiction Writing Toolkit: Resources and Insights for Fiction Writers".

Hello, introverts. What you are about to read will likely change the way you view networking. I start with some clarifying definitions. Don't skip them. I believe there's liberation in these re-definitions of introversion.

Introversion is not the same as shyness. Being

shy means you avoid social settings because you are nervous or timid. Anyone can suffer from a bit of timidity from time to time, even an extrovert. Being an introvert means you draw energy and deep satisfaction from your own solitary personal interests and thoughts. Introversion is a temperament, a permanent part of a person's nature. It's neither good nor bad. It's just how you are. Accept it. Embrace it. And learn how to leverage it to the advantage of your life and the lives around you.

I am an introvert. When I take those temperament surveys, I test out near or at 100% introvert. I've been practicing some of the networking methods below for the better part of a decade. There is no guarantee they will work for you, but they are free for the taking. In addition, they are easy to master. Applying them consistently and properly is totally up to you. And just in case you're wondering, you can use them if you're an extrovert as well.

Here's a little more about me, the 100% introvert. I ran a multimillion-dollar statewide grant program for almost five years. And for over two years, I taught university engineering classes while advising approximately 100 students a semester and directing a mentoring program for first-year engineering students. I owned and operated a one-woman web design company, serving colleges and small businesses for over a decade prior to that. I've appeared on TV and radio several times. I've even been called a "people person". Not bad for a person who used to get sick to her stomach at the thought of speaking in public.

You might ask: What turned me into such an "extrovert"? I didn't turn into an extrovert. I practiced a few techniques I learned from observing extroverts and other introverts. Study and practice were key, despite some failures along the way.

Enough preamble. Here's my list of advice:

- Prepare for Interaction
- Practice Recharging Self-care
- Make a Habit of Affirming Yourself
- Follow a Script
- Get Out There

Allow me to unpack each of these items, one by one.

PREPARE FOR INTERACTION

When I mention "business networking", you probably envision a hundred or more business owners attending a business chamber function in a hotel meeting room, swapping business cards like a bunch of talking heads. That's one type of business networking. But it can also include having lunch with a business peer, participating in community charity functions, and interacting on a local business Facebook group. Whatever the networking vehicle, you must prepare yourself to get behind the wheel and drive it. Don't leave your networking to chance.

Networking is inevitable. Spend time preparing yourself for success. I don't care for the fake-it-till-you-make-it mindset. People can tell when you're faking. And most of all, you know when you're faking. Nothing drains me more than being fake. Introverts are good at in-depth study and investigation. We'll analyze a thing to death before we do it.

Use your natural tendencies to your advantage. Make a long hard study of public speaking and networking. Use Google. Search YouTube. Attend free talks given by famous speakers and take notes. The skills you learn in studying others can be applied in other areas of your life. For instance, public speaking and networking skills that I learned from the business and engineering world served me when I had to market my books. I knew I could not be fake at a book reading. I had to truly feel comfortable speaking at Barnes and Noble's book readings where I didn't know a soul. I had to exude confidence when I visited a book club meeting with the church ladies I'd met on social media. I *was* 'the event' so I had to be genuinely me and engaging.

I made public confidence my goal. It might sound silly to you, particularly if you are an extrovert. Each year, I write out my goals. I'm not the type to make New Year's resolutions. I write detailed goals. One year I listed my self-development goals, placing public confidence at the top of the list. I recorded video and audio of myself. I wrote out interview questions and practiced my answers with a stuffed-toy audience (they were my kid's stuffed toys, okay). I studied successful PR people and copied their techniques.

Succeeding as an introvert in an extrovert-centric world means pushing through the rough spots because there will be times when you mess up. In fact, expect to drop the ball, to go brain-dead in front of lots of people and to say something stupid. Your first few times will most likely be awful. Get over it. You'll live and learn.

PRACTICE RECHARGING SELF-CARE

Most of all, introverts need time to recharge between energy-draining events. I recharge by being *by myself* with a good book, taking a quiet walk *by myself*, or doing something creative like knitting or drawing *by myself*. See the pattern here? If I don't make time to charge up, I will crash and burn.

Protect this downtime. I've heard some folks like Michael Hyatt say they put their downtime on their appointment calendars. Did you catch that? Michael Hyatt, who happens to be a successful blogger and business coach (check out MichaelHyatt.com), makes an appointment with himself. I love that thought. Treat yourself like you're important because you are.

This leads to my next piece of advice: self-care.

Much of my self-care involves pulling my creative side out of hiding. It is an intentional exercise. I don't wait for 'inspiration' to start painting, drawing, or writing. With relish, I close the door on the world and make time for me.

For some introverts that 'me' time might take on a more physical dimension. Maybe you like to explore the great outdoors and hike or bike. Don't be ashamed to do this alone but do be safe. Carry your cell phone, pepper spray, and house/car keys. Always be aware of your surroundings and never go out alone at night.

This might not be the case for all introverts, but I lean toward the adventurous. I've taken my introverted self on hikes along parts of the Appalachian Trail as well as on walks in the so-called rough neighborhoods of Chicago, Atlanta, New York City, Washington D.C., and St. Louis.

During those walks, I've cleared my head, learned something new about my country and her people, and even come up with new ideas for my business or my books.

During your 'me' time, always have a spiral notebook or journal on hand. Jot down any new business ideas that come to you. Trust me, they will come. That's the way you're wired.

MAKE A HABIT OF AFFIRMING YOURSELF

Extroverts get energized by having people around them. They LOVE group work and get most of their ideas while working with others. They've found their sweet spot in the melee. Meanwhile, you can barely remember your name much less come up with a new idea for increasing business sales when things stay rowdy for hours.

All introverts have had those moments. The times when you pull up short on ideas and inspiration has taken a long vacation. I want you to promise me something right now. During these moments, you will follow my next piece of advice: affirm yourself.

You read that correctly. I want you to affirm YOU. In fact, take a moment to print the affirmations below on a note card or sticky note. Or better yet, type them into a note on your cell phone. And when you're in a stressful situation and tempted to put yourself down because all the quick to the draw, verbal extroverts are looking intelligent and innovative and successful,

Repeat after me:

- I belong here.
- I am capable.
- I am worthwhile.
- I am valuable.

Having written affirmations is a good way to remind yourself of your worth and your greatness. Add a SWOT analysis to the affirming mix. A SWOT analysis lists your strengths, weaknesses, opportunities, and threats to your business. Google it for more information and samples.

FOLLOW A SCRIPT

Another strategy to use to show your networking buddies just how great you truly are is to get a meeting or conference agenda up front. This way, you won't be blindsided by the format and content of the meeting. Take the time before the meeting to prepare what you will literally or figuratively bring to the table. Your prep time might take an hour or it might take a minute. It totally depends on what the meeting is about and how much you want to get out of it.

One crucial thing you'll bring to each and every business networking opportunity is your thirty-second elevator speech. Practice this self-intro in the mirror and give it to one or two trusted business friends beforehand. Hone it like your business depends on it because it does.

In fact, I found that scripting out my responses to typical conversations helped me immensely in the business world. A word of caution here. You're not going to have a script for conversations with your best friends. And you're not going to be looking at prompts on notecards. That would be totally stupid. As a fellow introvert, I would never want you to look stupid. Your rehearsal script is our little secret. No need for the extroverts to know what you've been up to. Once you're comfortable with your script, they might even mistake you for one of them. Like me, you might even be accused of being a 'people person'.

A typical script for an after-hours business mixer might go like this:

YOU: Hi. (extend hand to greet person you've

never met) My name is Linda Hargrove. How many of these events have you been to?

THEM: (shakes your hand and introduces him/herself)

YOU: I'm new here. My business is small, but we deliver high-quality affordable graphic design services. I specialize in serving the restaurant industry. You seem to know the lay of the land. Do you know if anyone here is in the market for my services?

This initial exchange is short and relatively painless. In a few seconds, you've not only delivered a short elevator speech, you've empowered a stranger to speak for you. And that's priceless. Of course, if this person comes up empty, politely excuse yourself, fake an important phone call, and try again with another person.

GET OUT THERE

Admittedly, contact with a perfect stranger at a mixer can be nerve-racking. Push past the initial fear and anxiety and do it anyway. It really comes down to who knows you. Join a business chamber and attend meetings. Once you've been there a few months, volunteer in a high visibility but low skills post. For instance, volunteer to man the door and hand out programs at the next business development talk. Help put out place cards or promotional items on tables when a famous keynote speaker comes to your city's convention center. Make it your business to know about these events and find out what the organizers need help with, then push past your fear and volunteer.

The more you show up and lend a hand, the more visible you become without having to say much. Extroverts get a seat at the proverbial table because of what they reveal through talking. You get a seat at the "table" based on what you reveal about yourself as a valuable resource. You could try taking yourself to the table like an extrovert, but you'll wear yourself out quickly and you'll probably come across as mean and anti-social while trying to be someone you're not. Because guess what, it shows. Especially, if this is your first time networking. Everyone can see that you feel uncomfortable and awkward.

Slowly but surely, you'll become known by a small group of people for the smart, funny, capable person that you are. And before long, they will be talking you up and opening doors for you. It's the old proverb. Your gifts will make room for you. It's not really who you know, it's who knows you.

BONUS FEATURE:

A few years ago, I was surfing TED.com for material to use in one of my freshman engineering classes and discovered a TED Talk that changed my way of looking at coping in a world of extroverts. It's a twenty-minute talk by Amy Cuddy entitled, "Your body language shapes who you are." In the video, social scientist Cuddy talks about increasing your perceived competence in social settings by making a two-minute posture change before an anxiety-producing encounter. She models what she calls power poses. Make a point of searching out her video this week. It can change the way you approach public appearances. http://www.ted.com/talks/
amy_cuddy_your_body_language_shapes_who_you_are

ABOUT THE AUTHOR

Linda Leigh Hargrove has been designing for web and print media for more than 15 years. She's an engineer, a multi-published fiction author, a mother of three boys, and a wife of more than 25 years. Linda is a North Carolina native and tinkers on 3D printers in her free time. Her life motto, "She is no fool who gives what she cannot keep to gain what she cannot lose", governs every business decision. Find out more about her work at 1721Media.com.

11

NETWORKING OPTIONS ON SOCIAL MEDIA

AUDREY TYLER

Let's face it human beings want to connect with another human being in a meaningful way. Networking is one of the most important connection building activities we can incorporate into our lives. Networking is an opportunity to elevate a conversation into a meaningful connection that offers value to you and the person you are networking with. It's hard to imagine networking without using social media, especially for the Millennial generation. The first generation born with no memory of life without the World

Wide Web, they live connected. According to a 2018 Pew Research Study, Baby Boomers grew up as television expanded dramatically, changing their lifestyles and connection to the world in fundamental ways. Generation X grew up as the computer revolution was taking hold, and Millennials came of age during the internet explosion.

In this progression, what is unique for post-Millennials is that all of the above have always been a part of their lives. The iPhone launched in 2007, when the oldest post-Millennials were ten years old. By the time they were in their teens, mobile devices, WiFi and high-bandwidth cellular service were the primary means by which young Americans connected with the web. Social media, the constant connectivity, on-demand entertainment and communication are innovations Millennials adapted to as they came of age.

We use social media for a variety of purposes. To make new friends, be notified about events, training and just staying connected to people with common interests. According to a 2018 Pew Research Study, around seven in ten Americans use social media to connect with one another, engage with news content, share information and entertain themselves. At the speed of light, we can connect with people beyond the border of our state and even our country. There are no boundaries or limits to how many relationships we can build when it comes to networking via social media. In the past, email, phone, and face-to-face were the only available ways to connect. Now, there are dozens of ways to connect. From teleconferencing to Facebook groups, the network building options available today are mind-boggling.

I personally participate in a bible study and a writer's social networking group on Facebook.

These groups allow individuals of different ages and stages from multiple states to come together and discuss common interests. In the writer's group, although we write in different genres, we comment on each other's blog posts, encourage each other in the writing process and offer prayer support. In the bible study group, we come together online to "gather" as Christ taught us, to praise, to help and to love one another.

How do you begin communicating via social media? How do you stay connected? What tools are essential for social network building? The mediums I use in my Facebook social networking groups are a great place to start:

- Connecting Live (Facebook Live)
- Live Training (Zoom)
- Make the Call (Teleconferencing Calls)
- Reach Out and Touch (face-to-face)

Connecting Live

The Facebook bible study group uses Facebook Live for group study. Facebook Live is a live video streaming service that allows Facebook users to broadcast from their devices straight to their Facebook News Feed. Facebook Live is another networking platform that assists in building authentic relationships with followers in real time.

Live Training

The writer's group uses Zoom for online training and meetings.

Zoom has some outstanding features:

- Screen sharing, content sharing
- Webinars, demo, tutorials

Zoom is an easy way to connect and disseminate training information. The group facilitator can evaluate the training needs of the group and develop a training schedule. An alternative to Zoom is GoToMeeting which operates on a similar platform. One benefit of live training is the ability to train multiple people who reside in various locations without anyone having to travel.

MAKE THE CALL

My bible study group uses the website, Free Conference Call, for our monthly teleconference call. This technology is available to anyone who has a phone. The specific purpose of the bible study group's teleconference call is to commune for prayer and share a fifteen-minute inspirational word. This is another way to network and strengthen one another. As an added benefit of participating as a speaker, people get to know you through your voice.

REACH OUT AND TOUCH

Before you rush to download these latest tools, heed this warning. Never let technology replace human touch. There is no technology that can replace face-to-face connection. Face-to-face connection adds value to your relationship. Whenever the groups I'm a member of meet in person, whether it be a writer's conference, retreat or a workshop, we have fun inspiring and committing to each other's success. If there are opportunities to meet in person, take the time to attend. The relationship will become more meaningful. Local meetups can be fun and exhilarating.

Here are some tidbits on what to do at a face-to-face event:

Don't be shy – Engage in conversations. Have a few questions for conversation starters. If everyone is wearing a name tag and the name tag states where they are from, you can start by saying, "I notice you're from South Carolina. Where at in South Carolina?" You may be amazed by the number of people from your state or nearby and the flood of opportunities for networking that can open up as a result of being from the same area.

Find common ground. Attending events with people you have common interests with allows you to share ideas, best practices — what is working and not working and new opportunities. One of my first writing opportunities came from a writer's workshop I attended in the beautiful mountains of Tennessee. The speaker, who is also an editor, approached me before leaving the workshop and said, "I want a story from you." I couldn't wait to get back home to start writing that story. As a result of attending that writer's workshop , I am now a published writer. Taking the time to attend events that pertain to your interest can be a huge payoff.

The love of reading and studying God's Word motivates me to connect with people. I want to be connected and learn as much as I can about studying and writing about God with like-minded individuals. The bible study group started out as a face-to-face meet up. When Facebook Live was introduced, the facilitator decided to use it to conduct the bible study and it has worked out well.

Using social media as a networking tool allows a group of people to come together, study, train and share their common interests in a short amount of time.

Social media tools are available to support your

networking efforts but to be effective you must connect. When connecting with groups with common interests you will find plenty of opportunities to meet like-minded people. Being part of a group with common interests can be a wonderful resource for information. You will make great friends and find people that can help you develop in your common interest area as it has done for me with bible study and writing.

If you are serious about connecting, strategize on how you can incorporate these social media tools into your networking efforts.

ABOUT THE AUTHOR

Audrey Tyler loves reading and studying God's word. She is contributing writer for her church newsletter and for non-fiction MOMENTS series, *Spoken Moments* and *Stupid Moments*, compiled and edited by author Yvonne Lehman.

OTHER BOOKS
IN THE SERIES

WHEN WOMEN BECOME BUSINESS OWNERS

A STEPPING INTO VICTORY COMPILATION: VOLUME 1

Are you a business owner? A freelancer? A stay-at-home mom? Are you still working a nine-to-five job, but dream of working for yourself?

There is great joy and risk to becoming an entrepreneur. This anthology seeks to provide hope for the journey and a roadmap for finding balance as an entrepreneur.

When Women Become Business Owners provides solid business and faith-based advice from real twenty-two female entrepreneurs. Find wisdom, inspiration, and encouragement for those times when you may find road blocks or fear trying to snatch your dream away.

Made in the USA
Middletown, DE
20 September 2018